Reading, Thinking, Writing

Reading, Thinking, Writing

A Text for Students of English as a Second Language

Mary S. Lawrence

Ann Arbor

The University of Michigan Press

ISBN 0-472-08548-4
Library of Congress Catalog Card No. 74-25946
Published in the United States of America by
The University of Michigan Press
Manufactured in the United States of America

1990 1989 1988 1987 16 15 14 13

For Jennifer,
who helped

Preface

This text is designed to teach the fundamentals of two basic communication skills: reading analytically and writing logically. It is intended for students who are still mastering elementary grammar patterns and should be used in conjunction with a standard grammar text, such as Krohn's *English Sentence Structure* published by The University of Michigan Press in 1971. It is based on the assumption that reading and writing are both thinking processes and that the primary aim of second language instruction in reading and writing skills should be to teach the student *how to go about* reading and writing, and to teach him in such a way that he can apply the procedure successfully after he leaves the second language program. This implies the necessity for a systematic approach with an underlying coherent method. The student's mastery of individual reading selections and individual composition assignments, therefore, is important only insofar as it reflects his increasing competence in learning *how* to read carefully and accurately to acquire information and in learning *how* to write logically and coherently.

If reading and writing are to be taught as processes, we should be able to explain exactly what the proficient reader does while he is reading, what the skillful writer does while he is writing. Unfortunately, we cannot, at this time, explain exactly what the processes of reading and writing entail—exactly what people do linguistically, psychologically, and physiologically when they write. On the other hand, it is hardly practical to wait for a perfect all-inclusive explanation of cognition before we try to teach ESL students reading and writing as a thinking process. The concept of thinking which underlies this text is that of Jerome S. Bruner as set forth in his book *Toward a Theory of Instruction* published by W. W. Norton and Company in 1968. The text focuses on three cognitive skills: the ability to make extrapolations; to manipulate and to impose order on data; and to synthesize data. These are thinking processes we all engage in daily. We all impose order on the multiplicity of data with which life confronts us. We all make mental leaps beyond the data at hand to form inferences and extrapolations of varying degrees of sophistication. We all combine and recombine data from more than one source. The materials in the text are organized to show the student how to apply these skills to the task of learning to read and write in a second language. In addition, materials in the exercises (grammar, vocabulary, and methods of logical organization) are spiralled to facilitate recall and transfer. The lessons are cumulative and sequenced to teach the student how to read critically and how to write coherently within the confines of his expanding linguistic competence.

Divided into eight units, the text provides ample practice and a wide variety of exercises and classroom activities. The lessons integrate reading and writing by focusing on the grammar and vocabulary of logical relationships.

Specific information for the teacher about basic principles, classroom procedures, and supplementary activities is given in the *Teacher's Manual.*

M. S. L.

Acknowledgments

This textbook is due in large measure to the encouragement of my colleagues at the English Language Institute at the University of Michigan, who expressed confidence that the method of teaching composition used in *Writing as a Thinking Process* could be applied to less proficient ESL (English as a second language) students. Almost all the composition teachers at the Institute contributed comments and suggestions. Particular thanks are due Carol Compton, Joanne Druist, John H. Esling, Daniel Grumbles, Dorothy Messerschmidt, Barbara McKinley, Johanna Wilson, Rita Wong, and Joyce Zuck. I am also indebted to my colleagues at the University of Toronto, the University of Ottawa, Algonquin College of Applied Arts and Technology, and the English Language Services in Washington D.C. for their comments and enthusiasm.

I wish to extend very special thanks to Laura Strowe, who drew the illustrations, and to Ginny Barnett, who typed and proofread the manuscript.

Introduction

To the Student

(*Read silently while your teacher reads aloud.*)

Please read this introduction *three* times: First, before you use this book. Next, in the middle of your course. Finally, when you have finished the textbook.

Students who are learning a second language are usually exceptionally intelligent people. You already know at least one language very well. You already know *how to think.* What you think is not the same as what your neighbor, or classmate, or other members of your family think, even when you have shared the same experiences. You each organize information about your experiences in different ways. Each of you–

1. makes some kind of logical sense out of your experiences and the many kinds of information you receive in your life;

2. makes inferences about people and events; forms ideas about what you read and what people tell you;

3. combines and recombines information from more than one source.

Although no two students have identical thoughts, each of you uses these three ways of thinking. This textbook asks you to use your ability to think in these three ways when you read and write in English:

1. to manipulate data according to logical relationships that are common in written English;

2. to make extrapolations (inferences);

3. to make syntheses (to combine data; to combine data and inferences; to combine methods of imposing logical order on data).

These are methods of thinking you use every day. You can use them to learn to read and write with increasing skill in English.

Many students think that learning vocabulary is the most important part of reading and that studying grammar is the best way to learn to write. Of course, it's impossible to read and write without knowing some grammar and vocabulary, but it is not necessary to know everything there is to know about English grammar and vocabulary to read intelligently or to express your ideas in English. In fact, native speakers, including English teachers, don't know everything about grammar and vocabulary. This textbook has grammar practice exercises, but they are only there to help you learn *how* to analyze what you read logically and *how* to organize what you write logically. The most important vocabulary and grammar in the book is the vocabulary and grammar of logical relationships–the sentence patterns, words, and phrases you need to think about what you are reading and what you are writing. Almost all of these grammar patterns are in your grammar textbook, but they are probably not in the same order. This is good because it gives you a chance to review the grammar you learn and use it in a new situation. In this book you will find the important vocabulary and grammar of logical relationships in boxes; please *learn* these words, phrases, and sentence patterns. Try to *recall* and *use* them. You will probably not remember the stories in this book for very long, but you should remember the vocabulary and grammar of logical relationships in the boxes and be able to use them long after you have finished this book.

Contents

UNIT 3

UNIT 4

Unit 1: Reading

The Neighbors

Miss Ann Johnson is twenty-seven years old. She lives alone in an apartment on Main Street. Her apartment is on the third floor. Miss Johnson is a musician. She plays the piano. She practices for two hours every day. She never plays the piano at home in the evening because she works in a nightclub. She seldom practices in the morning because she usually sleeps late. She usually sings and plays the piano in the afternoon after lunch.

Mr. Wallace is the owner of the apartment building. He lives on the first floor. He is an old man and seldom goes out. He is a retired banker. He is a little deaf, but he loves radio programs and television. He always turns on the radio early in the morning. He usually listens to the radio all morning and then turns on the TV after lunch. He never misses his favorite TV shows. He turns up his radio and TV because he is deaf. People in the street often hear the programs too.

A family of four lives on the second floor. Mr. Post is a teacher. He teaches English in a big high school. Mrs. Post is an engineer. She is Mr. Post's second wife. She doesn't like Mr. Post's two sons. She always criticizes them. The boys are Michael and James. Michael is sixteen years old and James is ten. She says the boys are lazy and noisy. They play records in the morning and after school every day. They like loud music. Mrs. Post usually feels sick in the morning because she has a headache. She hates noise.

The fourth apartment is on the top floor. It is empty now.

Exercise 1: Reading for Information

Read the following sentences. Indicate if the sentence is true or false according to the story. You may look at the story again. This time, skim (read fast to find the answer). If the story doesn't give you enough information, you have insufficient data.

Examples:

Mr. Wallace lives on the first floor.

True	False	Insufficient data
Yes, he does.		

Miss Johnson is deaf.

True	False	Insufficient data
	No, she isn't.	

Mr. Post is fat.

True	False	Insufficient data
		I don't know.

1. The pianist lives below the family of four.

________ True ________ False ________ Insufficient data

2. The owner of the building likes noise.

________ True ________ False ________ Insufficient data

3. Miss Johnson sings in a nightclub.

________ True ________ False ________ Insufficient data

4. Mrs. Post is critical of the two boys most of the time.

________ True ________ False ________ Insufficient data

5. Mr. Wallace listens to the radio every day.

________ True ________ False ________ Insufficient data

6. The musician seldom practices in the evening.

________ True ________ False ________ Insufficient data

7. The piano is on the second floor.

________ True ________ False ________ Insufficient data

8. Mrs. Post isn't deaf.

________ True ________ False ________ Insufficient data

9. Mr. Wallace is busy every morning.

________ True ________ False ________ Insufficient data

10. Miss Johnson sometimes sleeps late.

________ True ________ False ________ Insufficient data

11. Fifty percent of the apartments are noisy in the morning.

__________ True __________ False __________ Insufficient data

12. Seventy-five percent of the apartments are vacant.

__________ True __________ False __________ Insufficient data

13. Mr. Wallace seldom turns down his TV.

__________ True __________ False __________ Insufficient data

14. Michael and James are Mr. Post's stepsons.

__________ True __________ False __________ Insufficient data

15. Mr. Wallace is never deaf in the morning.

__________ True __________ False __________ Insufficient data

Exercise 2: Making Inferences

The story tells us facts about the neighbors in the apartment building. Think about the facts. Do you have your own ideas about the people in the story? Do you have opinions about them? What can you guess about them? Make *inferences* about the people in the story. Use your imagination.

A. 1. I think Mr. Post has a problem because ____.

2. I think Mrs. Post doesn't like Mr. Wallace because ____.

3. I think the fourth apartment is empty because ____.

4. I think Mr. Wallace has a problem because ____.

B. Talk about these questions in class.

1. Does Miss Johnson hear Mr. Wallace's radio in the morning?

2. Does Mr. Wallace hear the noisy boys in the second floor apartment?

3. Is Mrs. Post happy?

4. Is Mr. Post happy?

5. Is Mr. Wallace lonely?

Exercise 3: Generalizations and Examples

A. Complete the following paragraphs. Each paragraph starts with a general statement. Add examples to prove it.

1. In my opinion, Mrs. Post is not a good stepmother. For example, she ______________________________ ______________________________. She thinks ______________________________ ______________________________. She ______________________________.

2. Generally speaking, the apartment building on Main Street is very noisy. For example, ______________ ______________________________ every morning. ______________________________ ______________________________. ______________________________.

Generalizations

On the whole, – – – – – – – –.

Generally speaking, – – – – – –.

Basically, – – – – – – – – – –.

– – – – – – always – – – – – –.

– – – – – – – never – – – – – –.

In my opinion, – – – – – – –.

Examples

For example, – – – – – – – –.

– – – – – – –, for example.

Let me give you an example.

Exercise 4: Oral Practice

Practice this pattern orally. Repeat after your teacher.

I'm not very sleepy. I'm just a little sleepy.

hungry	unhappy	sorry
deaf	homesick	busy
noisy	excited	late
lame	thirsty	early
sick	cold	

We can't say: The room is just a little empty.

The room is just a little vacant.

The man is just a little dead.

Why?

Exercise 5: Logical Questions

Write questions for the following answers.

	Question	*Short Answer*
1.	________________________?	On the third floor.
2.	________________________?	Ten years old.
3.	________________________?	Mr. Wallace.
4.	________________________?	In a high school.
5.	________________________?	Because they are noisy.
6.	________________________?	In the afternoon.
7.	________________________?	The radio.
8.	________________________?	Yes, she does.
9.	________________________?	At home.
10.	________________________?	Two boys.

Exercise 6: Abbreviations

Mrs. Post reads the ads for apartments in the newspapers every day. Advertisements sometimes use abbreviations.

> For Rent: Lrg. apt. Fourth flr. Very quiet bldg. No pets. Two bedrm. Lrg. lvrm. Utl. pd. Unfrn. Gd. lctn. $220 per mo. Call 662-3940.

Match the abbreviation with the correct word.

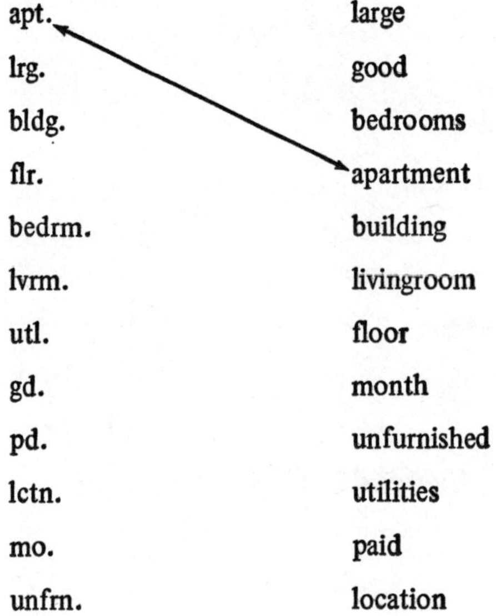

Conversation Practice

For Rent: Lrg. apt. Fourth flr. Very quiet bldg. No pets. Two bedrm. Lrg. lvrm. Utl. pd. Unfrn. Gd. lctn. $220 per mo. Call 662-3940.

Mrs. Post likes this ad. She wants a quiet apartment. She calls 662-3940.

Mr. X: Hello.

Mrs. Post: Hello? Is this 662-3940? Do you have an apartment for rent?

Mr. X: Yes, I do. It's a nice apartment.

Mrs. Post: Where is it?

Mr. X: On Main Street. It's a very convenient location, near the stores and the bus.

Mrs. Post: The apartment I live in is very noisy. I need a quiet apartment.

Mr. X: Speak up. I can't hear you.

Mrs. Post: I need a quiet apartment. Is your apartment quiet? Are the neighbors noisy?

Mr. X: Quiet? Of course it's quiet. The ad says so. Nobody is noisy here.

Mrs. Post: What is the address?

Mr. X: The apartment is at 961 Main Street. My name is Wallace. Come any time.

Mrs. Post: What? Did you say "Wallace"? (She hangs up the phone.)

Mr. Wallace: Hello. Hello. Speak up. I can't hear you.

Writing

Exercise 1: Writing Sentences

English sentences always start with a capital letter. They end with a period (.) or a question mark (?). Write sentences using the following words. You may change the order of the words.

Example:

stepmothers	critical of	usually	(?)

Are stepmothers usually critical of their stepchildren?

Are stepmothers usually critical of their quiet children?

1.	always	turn up	favorite	(.)
2.	noisy	seldom	floor	(.)
3.	neighbors	ever	criticize	(?)
4.	practice	musicians	usually	(.)
5.	retired	always	grandchildren	(?)
6.	old	often	deaf	(.)
7.	high school	floors	many	(?)
8.	hate	lazy	noisy	(.)
9.	mother	headache	morning	(.)
10.	floor	large	furnished	(?)

Exercise 2: Writing about Information—Generalizations and Examples

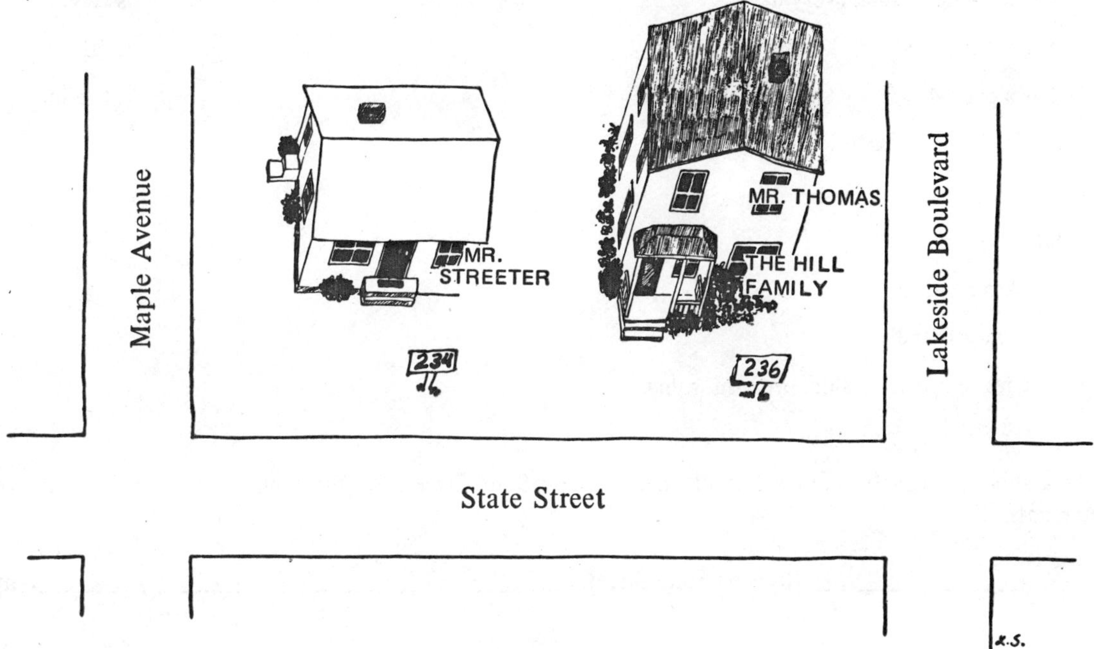

Information about Neighbors on State Street

Read the following information.

Mr. Streeter is 70 years old.
likes dogs.
hates cats.
doesn't work.
walks to the lake every day.
plays cards every Tuesday.
is friendly.
talks a lot about his grandchildren.

Mr. Streeter's dog is small.
chases cats.
barks every evening.
hates children.
bites mailmen.
digs holes.
is brown.

Mr. Thomas is 25 years old.
is a law student.
studies until 2 a.m.
is unfriendly.
is afraid of big dogs.
is Mr. Hill's brother-in-law.
hates smoke.

Mr. Hill is 30 years old.
is a mailman.
smokes a pipe.
plays in a jazz band.
plays the trumpet.
practices every evening.

Mrs. Hill is a housewife.
likes plants and flowers.
works in her garden every day.
is 25 years old.
has a pet cat.
is Mr. Thomas's sister.

Mrs. Hill's cat is black and white.
is very old.
is lazy.
is fat.
eats a lot.

Jimmy Hill is 3 years old.
likes animals.
is very friendly.
goes to nursery school every morning.

1. Write a short paragraph about a friendly neighbor on State Street. Be sure your examples prove your general statement.

__________ lives on State Street. __________ lives at __________ next to __________. Generally speaking, __________ is very friendly. __________ likes __________. __________ every day. __________ never criticizes __________. __________ seldom critical of __________.

2. Write a short paragraph about a pet animal on State Street. Be sure your examples prove your general statement.

__________ has a pet __________. It is __________, in my opinion. For example, __________. __________ likes it, but __________.

3. Write a short paragraph about an unhappy neighbor on State Street. Be sure your examples prove your general statement.

__________ lives at __________. In my opinion, __________ is usually unhappy. For example, __________ doesn't like __________. __________ is __________ and __________. __________ hates __________ and is __________ critical of __________.

Exercise 3: Writing Accurately about Information

Read the sentences. Is the information accurate? If the sentence is correct, copy it. If it is incorrect, write a new sentence with the correct information.

1. Mr. Thomas lives on the first floor and is Mrs. Hill's uncle.

____.

2. Mr. Thomas isn't afraid of Mr. Streeter's dog.

____.

3. Jimmy Hill is Mr. Thomas's nephew.

____.

4. Mr. Hill's mother-in-law is called Mrs. Thomas.

____.

5. Mr. Streeter is retired.

____.

6. Jimmy doesn't like Mr. Streeter's dog, but the dog likes him.

____.

7. Mr. Streeter and Mr. Thomas are friends.

____.

8. Mr. Streeter's dog doesn't like Mr. Hill.

____.

9. Mr. Streeter's home is on the corner of State Street and Lakeside Boulevard.

____.

10. The Hill family lives on State Street near a lake.

____.

Exercise 4: Using Apostrophes

Mr. Streeter has a dog. The dog is *Mr. Streeter's* dog. It digs holes in *Mr. Thomas's sister's* garden. Mrs. Hill is critical of the *dog's* holes. *Mr. Streeter's* pet hates mailmen. It bites the *mailmen's* legs. Mr. Hill criticizes the old *man's* pet.

Mr. Streeter has three friends. They play cards every Tuesday. They are noisy because the old man is a little deaf. *Mrs. Hill's* brother is critical of the *friends'* behavior.

Look at the above paragraphs.

What are the rules for forming the possessive?

What is the rule for people?

What is the rule for animals?

What is the rule for words that don't end in *s*?

What is the rule for words (not names) that end in *s*?

What is the rule for names that end in *s*?

Complete the following sentences.

1. Jimmy Hill is ____________________ son and ____________________ nephew.
2. Mr. ____________________ dog digs holes in ____________________ garden.
3. Mr. ____________________ neighbors live at ____________________.
4. ____________________ brother hates ____________________ dog because the ____________________ noise annoys him.
5. ____________________ pet always chases ____________________ pet.
6. ____________________ brother-in-law is unhappy because he is afraid of ____________________ pet, and he doesn't like ____________________ music.
7. Mr. Streeter says his dog bites ____________________ legs because five years ago it was afraid of a ____________________ uniform.

Exercise 5: Composition

A. Look at the story on page 1. How many paragraphs are there? Why?

B. Look at the information about the neighbors on State Street.

Write a composition about the two houses and their occupants.

How many paragraphs are you going to write?

What is your title going to be?

Don't copy the sentences in the book.

Use the information about the neighbors to make new sentences. Try to use new vocabulary from this lesson. Try to use generalizations and examples.

Exercise 6: Composition

Where do you live?

Who are your neighbors? What do they do? Do they work?

Where do they work? Are they noisy? What are their names?

Can you make some generalizations about them?

1. Make lists of information about your neighbors.
2. Write a composition about your neighbors. Use generalizations and examples.

Extra Vocabulary and Writing Practice

Exercise 1: Vocabulary Review

A. Practice the pronunciation of these words. Circle the words which refer to people.

Example: mail (mailman)

music	singer	location
musician	housewife	retiree
piano	friend	advertisement
pianist	partner	stepchildren
gardener	doctor	law
own	medicine	friendly
song	medical	advertise
owner	lawyer	smoker
teacher	assistant	

B. Give the correct form.

	noun	*adjective*
Example:	noise	noisy
	laziness	________________
	________________	quiet
	criticism	________________
	vacancy	________________
	________________	empty
	hunger	________________
	________________	musical
	________________	friendly
	excitement	________________
	________________	homesick
	fear	________________
	pet	________________
	________________	retired
	convenience	________________

Unit 1

Vocabulary and Writing

Exercise 2: Vocabulary and Spelling Review

Fill in the blanks. Each blank represents one letter.

1. Jimmy's m**other** is cr_ _ _ _ _ _ of Mr. Streeter's dog because it always d_ _ _ h_ _ _ _ in her g_rd_n.

2. Jimmy's _n_ _ _ always cr_t_c_ _ _ _ _ Mr. Hill be_ _ _ _ _ he is a m_s_c_ _ _ and sm_ _ _ _ a p_pe.

3. Mr. Streeter is a proud gr_ _ _f_ _ _ _ _ _, but his p_ _ dog d_ _ _ _'t _ _ _ _ ch_ _ _ren.

4. Main St. is always n_ _ _ _ in the m_ _ _ _ _ _.

5. The bl_ _ _ and _ _ _ _ _ cat never ch_ _ _ _ the _ _ _ _ _ _ d_ _ because it is _ _d and _ _t.

Exercise 3: Compositions

A. 1. Choose a friend or classmate. Ask questions about his house or apartment. Find out about his neighbors.

2. Make a list of this information. Can you make some generalizations about the neighbors? Can you support the generalizations with examples?

3. Use the information to write a composition about your friend's neighbors.

B. Write a composition about an annoying neighbor. What does an annoying neighbor always do? What does an annoying neighbor never do? Does he have pets, children, a piano, etc.? Is he usually noisy, critical, unfriendly, etc.? Does he borrow money? Does he play a drum at midnight? Use the vocabulary in this lesson. Start your composition with a generalization.

C. Write a composition about the people in a noisy apartment building. Make a list of information first. Use generalizations and examples. Be sure your examples support your general statement.

Unit 2: Reading

A Newspaper Reporter Reports about Himself

I'm a newspaper reporter. I don't have much money, but I meet a lot of interesting people. Some are rich; others are poor. One or two are dishonest, but the others tell the truth most of the time. On the whole, I like my job, and I am good at it. I type fast. I have a good memory. I don't talk a lot, but I'm a good listener. I'm probably the best listener in the entire city, and I look stupid. I have a very stupid face. People look at me, and then they explain things to me very slowly. Other reporters ask people a lot of questions and make them angry, but I just look stupid and soon I am getting a lot of information: many uninteresting opinions, many irrelevant facts, but always a little interesting news for my column.

I have a method for getting news from the ordinary man in the street. Let me give you an example. Yesterday afternoon I needed information about recreation for elderly poor people in the city. I went to the park, sat on a bench in the sun, and waited. Soon, an old lady came and sat next to me. She carried two large paper bags and an old handbag. I sat quietly beside her for about ten minutes, and then I unwrapped a chocolate bar slowly. I made a lot of noise with the paper wrapping. Next, I offered her a piece of my chocolate. After that, she told me about herself. She doesn't have any real home. She and two friends sleep in the bus station; on warm days she comes to the park with her few belongings in two paper bags. Later, we went to a restaurant for a cup of coffee and a sandwich. I paid, of course. I didn't take any notes. I asked her a few questions about recreation, but she wasn't interested in that. She needed money and a place to live, she said. She told me a lot about the bus station. I gave her a dollar and some change. Finally, I left her in the park, went back to the office, and typed up some notes for my column.

Exercise 1: Reading for Information

Read the following sentences. Indicate if the statement is true or false according to the story.

Example:

The old lady in the story liked the bus station.

Yes, she did.	*No, she didn't.*	*I don't know.*
True	False	Insufficient data

1. Reporters usually ask too many questions.

______	______	______
True	False	Insufficient data

2. The old lady in the story was often hungry.

______	______	______
True	False	Insufficient data

3. The reporter didn't get any relevant information for his column from the old lady.

| __________ True | __________ False | __________ Insufficient data |

4. The town needed more recreational facilities for old people.

| __________ True | __________ False | __________ Insufficient data |

5. People rarely tell the truth, according to the reporter in the story.

| __________ True | __________ False | __________ Insufficient data |

6. This reporter is a kind person.

| __________ True | __________ False | __________ Insufficient data |

7. This reporter is a man.

| __________ True | __________ False | __________ Insufficient data |

8. Recreation for poor people is an important question in the reporter's city.

| __________ True | __________ False | __________ Insufficient data |

9. This reporter wastes a lot of time.

| __________ True | __________ False | __________ Insufficient data |

10. This reporter's method is always successful.

| __________ True | __________ False | __________ Insufficient data |

Exercise 2: Making Inferences

A. The story gives us information, but it doesn't tell us everything. We can guess additional information. Complete the following sentences. Give your ideas about the story. Make inferences.

1. I think the reporter is clever because ____
____.

2. In my opinion, the reporter is very stupid and inefficient because ______________________
____.

3. The old woman's story wasn't important for the reporter's column because ________________
____.

4. In my opinion, the old woman talked to the reporter because __________________________
____.

5. I think the reporter's boss is probably going to criticize him because ___________________
____.

B. Discuss the following questions about the story. Make inferences. Give your ideas.

1. Why did the reporter go to the park?
2. Was the reporter hungry? Why did he eat a candy bar?
3. Why did he unwrap the candy bar noisily?
4. Was the old woman dishonest?
5. Is recreation an important problem for the elderly poor? What problems are important?

Exercise 3: Logical Questions

Write the appropriate question for the following answers.

	Questions	*Short Answer*
1.	______________________________?	A sunny day.
2.	______________________________?	In the bus station.
3.	______________________________?	Noisily.
4.	______________________________?	A stupid one.
5.	______________________________?	Fast.
6.	______________________________?	On a bench.
7.	______________________________?	A cup of coffee.
8.	______________________________?	Back to the office.
9.	______________________________?	About recreation.
10.	______________________________?	His notes.

Exercise 4: Oral Practice

A. Practice this pattern orally.

The reporter looked stupid.	He looked like a stupid person.
My friend looks intelligent.	My friend looks like an intelligent person.
kind.	a kind person.
sad.	a sad person.
unhappy.	an unhappy person.
homesick.	a homesick person.
worried.	a worried person
sick.	a sick person.
healthy.	a healthy person.
bad tempered.	a bad tempered person.
angry.	an angry person.

B. Practice these patterns.

Some reporters make people feel angry.
them feel angry.
Some reporters make people angry.
them angry.

My friend made me (feel) unhappy.
glad.
homesick.
hopeful.
worried.
relaxed.
excited.
nervous.
tired.
sleepy.

Exercise 5: Chronological Order

A. Read the story again. Answer the following questions. Think about *when* events happened in the story. Chronological order is time order.

1. First, the reporter went to the park. What did he do next? Next, he ______________________

____.

2. He unwrapped his candy bar. What did he do after that? After that, he ______________________

____.

3. The reporter and the old lady talked in the park. Afterward, what did they do? Afterward, they ________

____.

4. The reporter sat quietly beside the old lady. Then, what did he do? Then, he ______________________

____.

5. The old lady took a piece of chocolate. What did she do after that? After that, she ______________

____.

6. They went into the restaurant. What did they do next? Next, they ______________________________

____.

7. The reporter left the restaurant with the old lady. Finally, what did they do? Finally, he

____.

Finally, she ____.

B. Which time word do we use first in a series? Which time word is always the last in a series? Which time words are used in the middle?

next	later	first
afterward	soon	after that
finally	then	

Exercise 6: Quoted Speech

A. Who is speaking? Read the following sentences and questions. Decide who is speaking.

Example:

"Do you like chocolate?" ___*the reporter*___ asked.

The reporter is speaking to the old woman in the park.

The reporter is asking the old woman a question in the park.

---

1. "The benches are hard, but it's warm and safe there," ______________________ said.

______________________ is speaking to ______________________.

______________________ is telling ______________________ about ______________________.

2. "Where do you keep your clothes?" ______________________ asked.

______________________ is speaking to ______________________.

______________________ is asking ______________________ a question ______________________

______________.

3. "Why are you asking me that? That's not important. Houses and food are important."

    ______________________ is speaking to ______________________ in the ______________________

    __________.

    ______________________ is answering ______________________'s questions about __________

    __________ in the ______________________.

    ______________________ is complaining to ______________________ about __________

    __________.

    ______________________ is telling ______________________ about ______________________.

4. "I like the summer best. It's sunny in the park. Sometimes I find a dime or an old sandwich,"

    ______________________ explained.

    ______________________ is speaking to ______________________ in the ______________________

    __________.

    ______________________ is telling ______________________ about ______________________.

5. "They all died years ago," ______________________ said.

    ______________________ is speaking to ______________________ about ______________________

    __________.

    ______________________ is telling ______________________ about ______________________.

6. "You want the newspaper to pay for two cups of coffee. Why was coffee necessary? You make me sick. You are stupid and inefficient. You waste a lot of time. What work did you do today?"

    ______________________ is speaking to ______________________.

    ______________________ is complaining to ______________________ about ______________________

    __________.

B. Study these patterns.

____________ is speaking to ____________ about ____________.

____________ is telling ____________ about ____________.

____________ is complaining to ____________ about ____________.

____________ is asking ____________ a question about ____________.

____________ is answering ____________'s question about ____________.

Learn these patterns

speak to somebody about – – – – –

complain to somebody about – – –

tell somebody about – – – – – – –

ask somebody about – – – – – – –

answer a question about – – – – –

Conversation Practice

The reporter walks home from work through the park every day. He sometimes stops and chats with the park policeman.

Policeman: Where's your girlfriend?

Reporter: Who do you mean? What girlfriend?

Policeman: The one with the paper bags. I mean old Sally. I watched you with her today over on that bench. You were giving her something. Was she asking for money?

Reporter: So her name is Sally, is it? She didn't tell me her name. No, she didn't ask for money. I was asking her some questions–for my column, you know. She's a funny old girl. Do you know much about her?

Policeman: She's an old nuisance, that's what she is. There are three of them. They are driving us crazy. The men at the bus station throw them out, but they turn up like bad pennies. They are hopeless. Did I tell you there are three of them? They sleep on the benches and make the customers nervous. Two people complained about them this morning.

Reporter: Do you know anything about Sally's family?

Policeman: Family? I don't know them, but they're no good. I know that. Why don't they keep her at home? Why don't they take care of her? She bothers decent folks, wastes the policemen's time, wastes taxpayers' money. They make me furious. They are no good. That's my opinion. I know. . . .

Reporter (interrupts him): Does she have any money?

Policeman: Don't ask me. She probably has a million dollars in her paper sacks. Say, why don't you write a column about it? Tell them all about it. Mention me in your column. I won't even charge you for the idea.

Writing

Exercise 1: Writing Sentences

Write sentences using the following words. Check your punctuation. How do you punctuate a question? How do you punctuate a statement? Note: You may change the order of the words.

Example:

	opinion	method	successful	(?)

In your opinion, was the reporter's method successful?

1.	elderly	interested	recreation	(?)
2.	listen	irrelevant	everyday	(.)
3.	Why	critical	family	(?)
4.	policemen	made	nervous	(.)
5.	inefficient	waste	taxpayers'	(.)
6.	old	turns up	penny	(.)
7.	customers	look at	station	(?)
8.	Why	take	notes	(?)
9.	policemen	watch	park	(.)
10.	complain	reporter	about	(?)

Exercise 2: Writing Paragraphs—Chronological Order

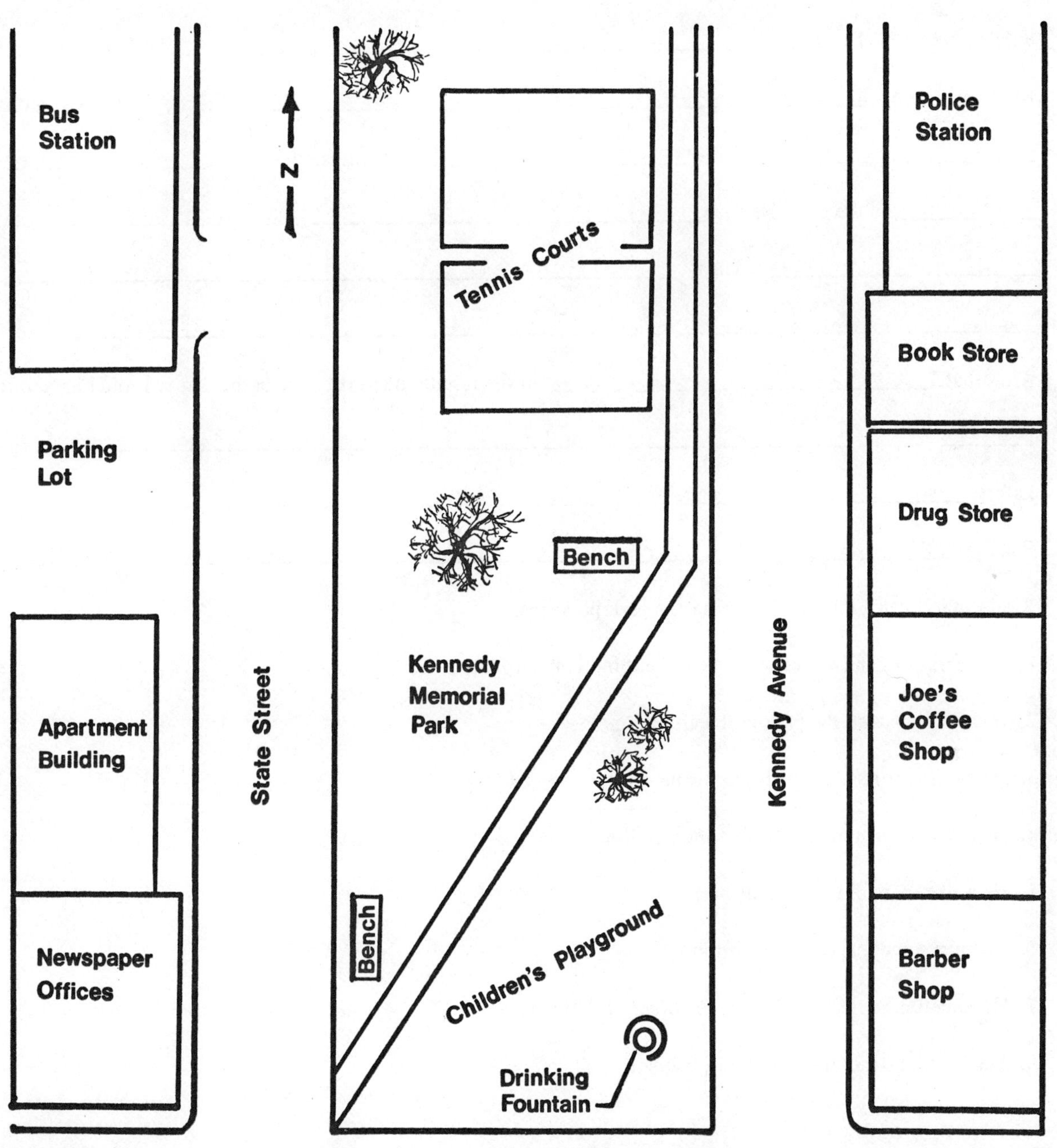

Unit 2
Writing

A. You are the old woman in the story. Yesterday you met the reporter. Use the information in the story and the map to write a paragraph about yesterday. Use chronological order (order in time).

My name is ______________________. I usually sleep ______________________ with my two friends. On sunny afternoons, I go ______________________ and ______________________. Yesterday, a policeman chased ______________________ out of ______________________ in the afternoon. I took my two ______________________ and ______________________. First, I walked along ______________________ to the ______________________ and crossed ______________________ ______________ to the park. Next, ______________________ ______________________. Then, ______________________ ______________________.

After that, ______________________ in the restaurant next to the barber shop. I told him about ______________________.

Later, ______________________.

Finally, ______________________.

B. Read the following information about the park policeman.

1. The park policeman lives in the apartment building on State Street.

2. He usually patrols the park in the afternoon.

3. He types reports in his office in the morning.

4. He eats his lunch in Joe's coffee shop at noon.

5. He walks to work through the park.

6. He buys a newspaper every morning.

7. He sometimes directs traffic at the corner of State Street and Park Avenue from 4 p.m. to 5 p.m.

8. Yesterday, he met the reporter in the park.

Use this information and information from the conversation practice dialog to write a paragraph about the policeman. Use chronological order for your paragraph.

Chronological Order

First, ––––––.

Next, ––––––.

Then, – – – – –.

After that, ––––.

Afterward, ––––.

Later, – – – – –.

Finally, ––––––.

Exercise 3: Writing Paragraphs—Generalizations and Chronological Examples

A. You are the owner of the newspaper. You think the reporter is lazy and stupid. Write a paragraph about your opinion. Start with a generalization. Think of relevant examples. Give your examples in chronological order.

Generalization: On the whole, John ________.

Examples: Yesterday, for example, __________.

First, ______. Next, ______, etc.

Conclusion: He makes me ______. I am going to fire him next week.

B. You are the reporter's girl friend. You think the reporter is kind. Write a paragraph about your opinion. Start with a generalization. Think of relevant examples from the story. Give your examples in chronological order.

Generalization: On the whole, John is a very kind man.

Examples: Let me give you an example. Yesterday ____.

First, ______. Next, ______, etc.

Conclusion: I like John because he makes people feel ______.

Exercise 4: Direct Speech

A. Read the following sentences. Look carefully at the punctuation. The sentences give the exact words of the speaker. This is called *direct speech.*

1. The reporter said, " She looks poor and hungry. "
2. The reporter asked, " Would you like a cup of coffee? "
3. " They sleep at the bus station, " the policeman said.
4. " Where is her family? " he asked.

B. Look at the following "sentences." They are all direct speech, but they aren't good sentences. They have no punctuation.

Write the sentences with the correct punctuation.

Example:

my family is dead she said sadly

"My family is dead," she said sadly.

---

1. where do you keep your clothes and your belongings he asked

2. they are a terrible nuisance at the bus station they make the customers nervous the policeman complained

3. she asked can I order a sandwich with my cup of coffee

4. food and housing are important she said

5. the reporter's boss said you look stupid and you are stupid you waste my time and my money

WET PAINT!

BUDDY'S GROCERY
EXIT
Special Today Eggs 65¢/doz
Buddy's Ground Coffee 1.05/lb.
Bread 50¢/loaf
Cereal
Bread
Peas
Soup
Corn
Eggs
Buddy's Ground Coffee

Exercise 5: Writing about Information—Generalizations and Chronological Order

Look at the pictures. Make inferences about the man in the pictures. What kind of a person is he? Discuss your ideas in class.

A. Complete the following paragraph. The paragraph starts with generalizations. Give examples. Use chronological order. Here is some vocabulary you can use. Ask your teacher for other words you need.

strong enough	tray	serve
too weak	leave a tip	spill
burst	tip a waiter	striped
break	restaurant	stripes

According to my mother, I'm a careless person, but that isn't true. She always says, "Roger, you are the most careless boy in the family." I am not careless. I'm careful, but I'm unlucky. Let me tell you about yesterday. Yesterday was a very unlucky day. First, ______________________________

____

____

____

____

____

____

____

____

____

____

____

B. Look at the pictures. You are the owner of the restaurant. What is your opinion about the man in the pictures?

1. Complete the following generalizations. Make inferences. Choose vocabulary from this list.

stupid	inefficient	intelligent
clumsy	careful	unfortunate
careless	competent	polite

a. On the whole, Roger ______________________________

b. In my opinion, Roger ______________________________

c. Generally speaking, Roger ______________________________

2. How does Roger make the restaurant owner feel? Make inferences. Choose vocabulary from this list.

nervous	relaxed	unhappy
angry	irritable	worried
intelligent	old	careful

a. He makes me feel ______________________________.

b. Last night he made me ______________________________

because he ______________________________.

c. He makes me feel ______________________________

because he ______________________________.

3. Complete the following letter.

March 10, 1974

Dear Mother,

I have a new waiter. He looks like an efficient person, but on the whole, he is stupid and clumsy. Yesterday, for example, he

Your loving son,

Extra Vocabulary and Writing Practice

Exercise 1: Vocabulary Review

A. The reporter wanted relevant facts, but he sometimes got irrelevant information. The adjectives *relevant* and *irrelevant* are opposites.

Match the pairs which have opposite meanings.

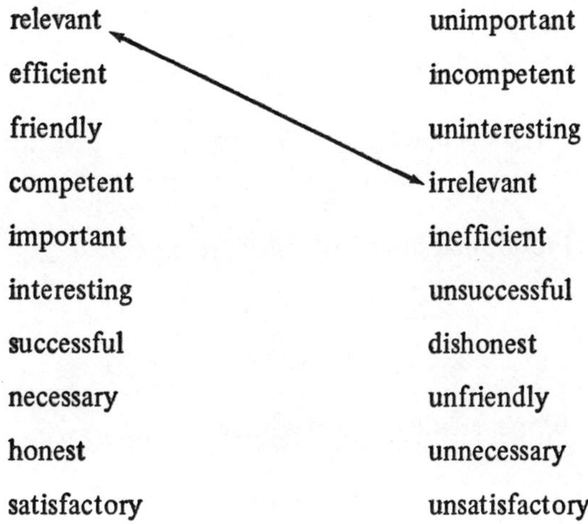

relevant	unimportant
efficient	incompetent
friendly	uninteresting
competent	irrelevant
important	inefficient
interesting	unsuccessful
successful	dishonest
necessary	unfriendly
honest	unnecessary
satisfactory	unsatisfactory

B. Practice the pronunciation of the pairs of words. Repeat the pronunciation after your teacher.

C. The old woman was a poor person. The reporter wanted information about the poor.

The poor means *poor people.*

Complete the following pairs.

Adjective	*Group Noun for People*
____________	the wealthy
____________	the living
dead	____________
old	____________
ill	____________
sick	____________
____________	the well
____________	the healthy
____________	the elderly
____________	the young
rich	____________

Exercise 2: Vocabulary and Spelling Review

1. The reporter un_ _ _ _ _ _ed his chocol_ _ _ candy bar and _ _ _ered a p_ _ce to the old lady.

2. The old wo_ _ _ always car_ _ _ _ all her belong_ _ _ _ in t_ _ paper bags from the bus _ _ _ _ion to the park on sun_ _ day_.

3. The reporter didn't always get re_ _ _ant inform_ _ _ _ _ for his _ _ _ _paper col_ _ _, but he lis_ _ _ed to a lot of in_ _ _ _ _ _ing _ _ _est people.

4. The _ _ _erly need houses and food first; after that, they are interested _ _ rec_ _ _tion, ac_ _ _ _ing to the old woman.

5. In my op_ _ _ _ _, clum_ _ people aren't _ _lucky; they are usually _ _ _ _less and in_ _ _pet_ _ _. I always com_ _ _ _ _ about un_ _ _ _ _fact_ _ _ service in res_ _ _ _ants and never _ _ve any tip.

Exercise 3: Compositions

A. Write a composition about a stupid, lazy person.

1. Start with a generalization.

   On the whole, – – – – – – – – –.

   or

   In my opinion, – – – – – – – –.

   or

   Generally speaking, – – – – – –.

   or

   Basically, – – – – – – – – – – –.

2. Prove your generalization with examples in chronological order. Use the past tense. Describe what he/she did yesterday. Make a list first. Then write your composition.

   a. Yesterday, for example, he/she – – –.

   or

   Let me tell you about yesterday.

   or

   Let me give you an example.

   b. First, – – –.

   Then, – – – –.

   Next, – – – –.

   After that, – – –.

   Afterward, – – –.

   Finally, – – – –.

3. Tell why you like/dislike this person.

   Use *complain about*

   makes me (feel)

B. Write a composition about a friend or member of your family who is a very busy person. Start with a generalization. Prove your generalization with examples. Describe one day in the person's life. Use chronological order.

C. Think about yourself. What kind of a person are you? Are you careful or careless? Prove you are a careful/careless kind of person with examples about one day in your life. Make a list first. Then arrange your list in chronological order. After that, write your composition. Start with a generalization.

Unit 3: Reading

The College Library

There are two big black and white signs on the wall beside the college library door.

No Smoking

No Eating

No Drinking

College Library Hours	
Mon. thru Fri.	8 a.m.–10 p.m.
Sat.	9 a.m.–5 p.m.
Sun.	2 p.m.–10 p.m.

Sometimes the students are so eager to study that they get to the library before it opens. This is not unusual during examination week. Once the doors are open, the students walk through a turnstile immediately in front of the door. The library with its carpeted floors is peaceful and quiet even on very busy days.

To the right of the doors there are shelves with current periodicals. The librarian arranges the new issues on these shelves so that the students can see the front covers of the current magazines. The colorful display of covers looks like an art gallery. Daily newspapers are also in this area, but they hang from sticks on special racks. There are eight comfortable easy chairs and two low tables nearby. The chairs are so comfortable that sometimes a student falls asleep. The library rules do not forbid sleeping.

The card catalog is in the middle of the room in front of the turnstile. There are always many students standing in front of the card catalog. Some are just chatting. Some are looking up books according to the author's name; others are looking for the names of books on a particular subject. They jot down the call numbers on scraps of paper. Without the proper call number, they can't find the books in the stacks.

The card catalog has hundreds and hundreds of cards. The cards are in alphabetical order according to the title of a book or periodical, the author, and the subject. Each book has a call number.

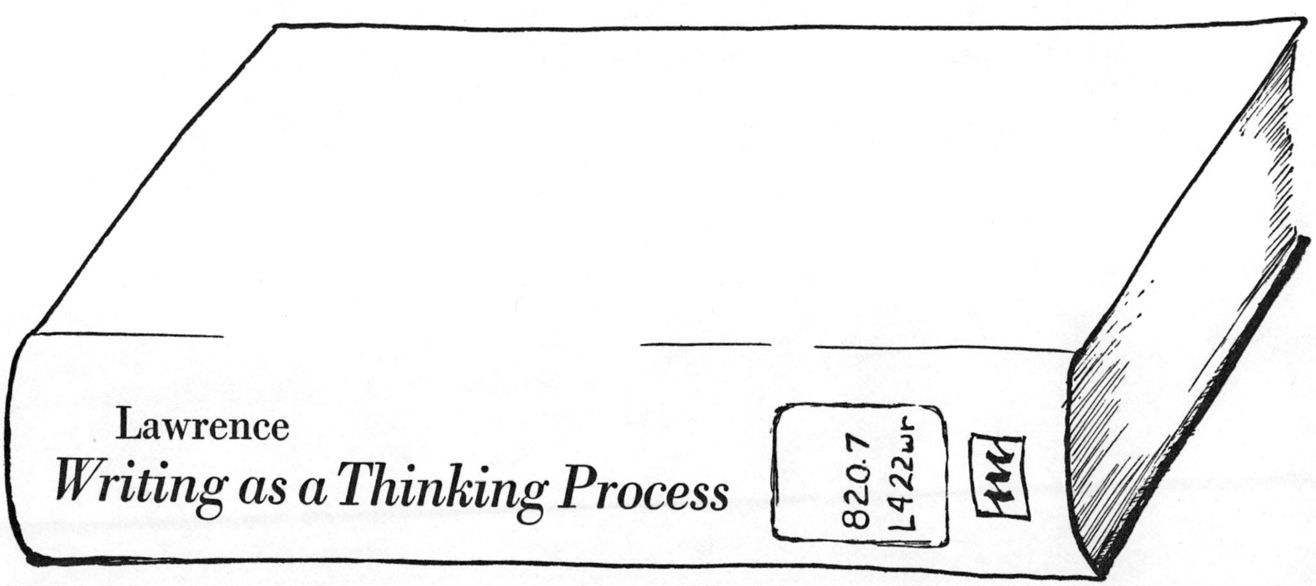

The books are on shelves, in order, according to the call numbers. The shelves are called the stacks. This library has open stacks so that the students can look for books themselves. The student must know the proper call number in order to find a book.

Every library has a reference desk and a circulation desk. The librarian at the reference desk answers questions. The circulation librarian checks out books. In order to check out a book the student must fill out a check-out slip.

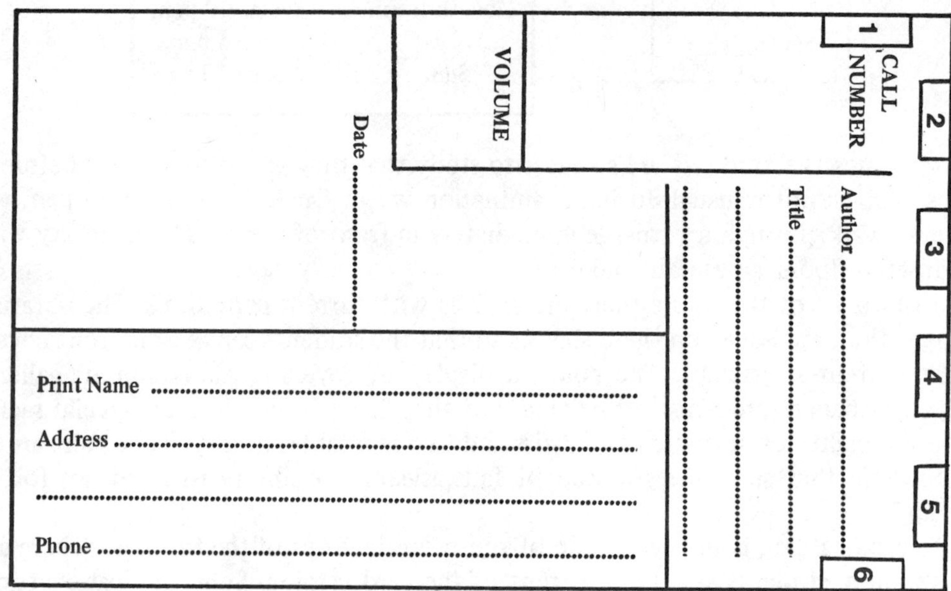

CALL NUMBER
VOLUME
Author ....
Title ....
Date ....
Print Name ....
Address ....
Phone ....
1
2
3
4
5
6

check-out slip

Students also return books to the circulation desk. Sometimes they must pay a fine. In the college library the fine is 25¢ a day for overdue books. Students can check books out for three weeks.

The college library has special equipment: tape recorders, slide projectors, microfilm readers, and videotape players. Some students copy pages from magazines and books on the photocopy machine. Each photocopy costs 10¢.

According to the librarian, the library is the most important part of the college.

Exercise 1: Reading for Information

Read the following sentences. Is the statement true according to the story? Is it false? Do you have enough information?

Example:

Overdue books cost 25¢ a week.

Yes, they do.	*No, they don't.*	*I need more information in order to know.*
True	False	Insufficient data

1. Every book has a different call number.

______	______	______
True	False	Insufficient data

2. The library rules forbid sleeping in the easy chairs.

______	______	______
True	False	Insufficient data

3. Only librarians can look for books in the open stacks.

______	______	______
True	False	Insufficient data

4. The library rules forbid talking in the library.

______	______	______
True	False	Insufficient data

5. Students must pay 25¢ for every check-out slip.

______	______	______
True	False	Insufficient data

6. The card catalog is in front of the door to the right of the turnstile.

______	______	______
True	False	Insufficient data

7. Students can relax in the area to the left of the card catalog.

______	______	______
True	False	Insufficient data

8. The reference desk is parallel to the card catalog immediately in front of the door.

__________ True   __________ False   __________ Insufficient data

9. A student can copy ten pages on the photocopy machine for a quarter or five nickels.

__________ True   __________ False   __________ Insufficient data

10. The books are on parallel shelves in alphabetical order in the stacks.

__________ True   __________ False   __________ Insufficient data

Exercise 2: Making Inferences

The story doesn't tell us everything about the library. Make inferences in order to answer the following questions.

1. Does the library have more than one librarian?

   In my opinion, __________

   because __________ .

2. Why did the college spend money for a carpet for the library floor? I think __________

   ____

   because __________ .

3. Are there any ashtrays on the tables in the library?

   __________ .

4. Why is there a turnstile in front of the door?

   __________ .

5. Why do some students complain about the overdue fine?

   __________ because

   __________ .

6. What question do new students often ask the librarian?

   New students often ask, "__________

   __________ ?"

Exercise 3: Logical Questions

You are a new student at the college. You have a lot of questions about the library. Read the following answers. Write the appropriate questions.

Example:

Question	*Short Answer*
When does the library shut on Saturdays?	At 5 p.m.
1. ______________________________?	To the right of the front door.
2. ______________________________?	The reference librarian.
3. ______________________________?	For three weeks.
4. ______________________________?	Ten cents a page.
5. ______________________________?	From 8 a.m. to 10 p.m.
6. ______________________________?	No, you can't.
7. ______________________________?	In order to find a book in the stacks.
8. ______________________________?	At the circulation desk.
9. ______________________________?	Look it up in the card catalog.
10. ______________________________?	On the racks beside the current magazines.

Exercise 4: The Card Catalog

A. Look at these three cards from the college card catalog.

The first card is *an author card.*

The second is *a title card.*

The third is *a subject card.*

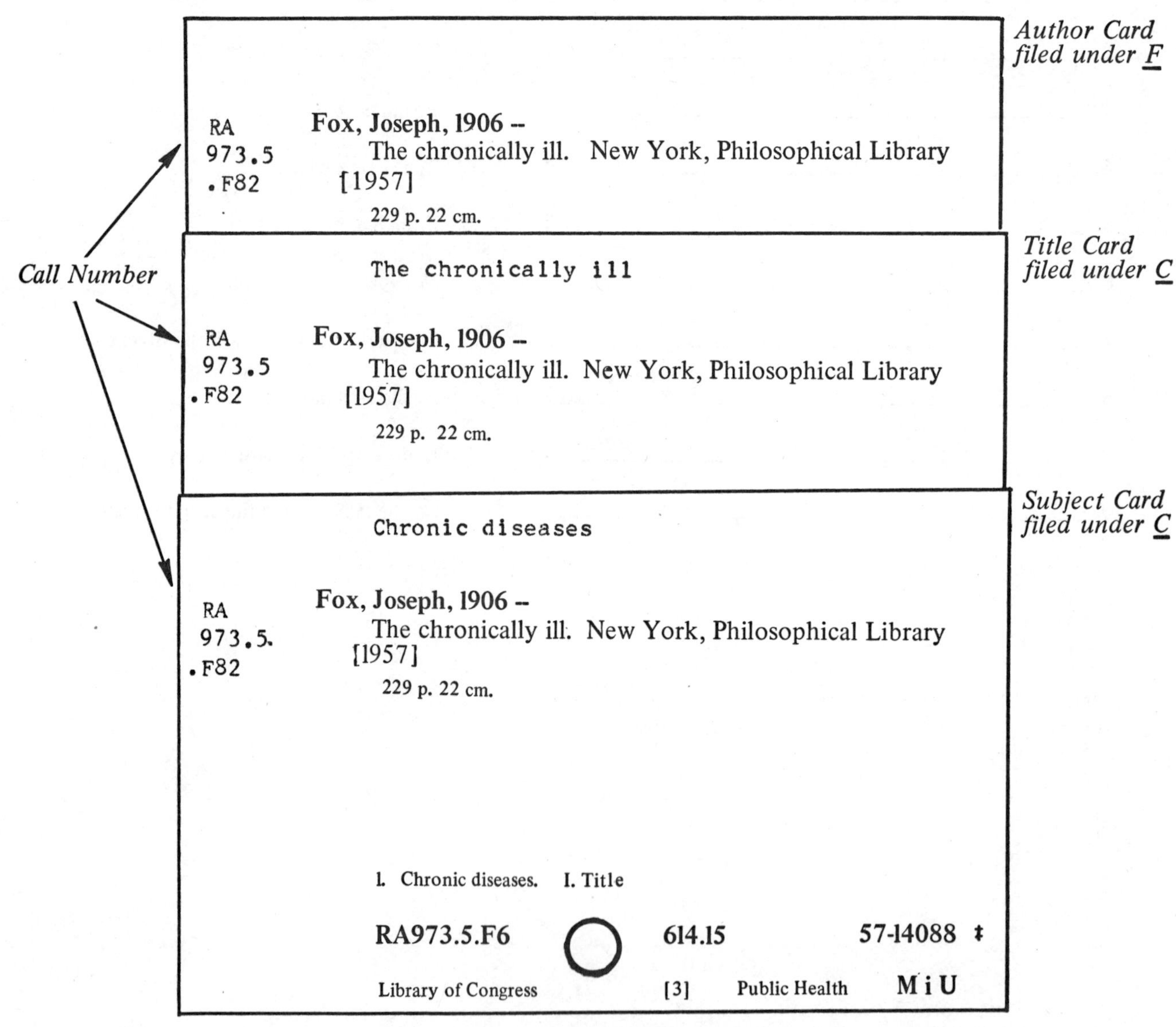

Each card gives: the author's name with family name first
the author's date of birth
the title of the book
the publisher of the book
the place and date of publication

1. Why is the author card in the F drawer of the card catalog?
2. How old is the author now?
3. How long ago was this book published? Where was it published?
4. Why is the title card filed under C? What rule does the library use for titles beginning with *the?* Why?
5. Sometimes the subject heading is exactly the same as the title. Sometimes they are different. Why?

B. Look at the following 10 cards from the card catalog. Answer the following questions. (Remember to underline the titles of books and periodicals.)

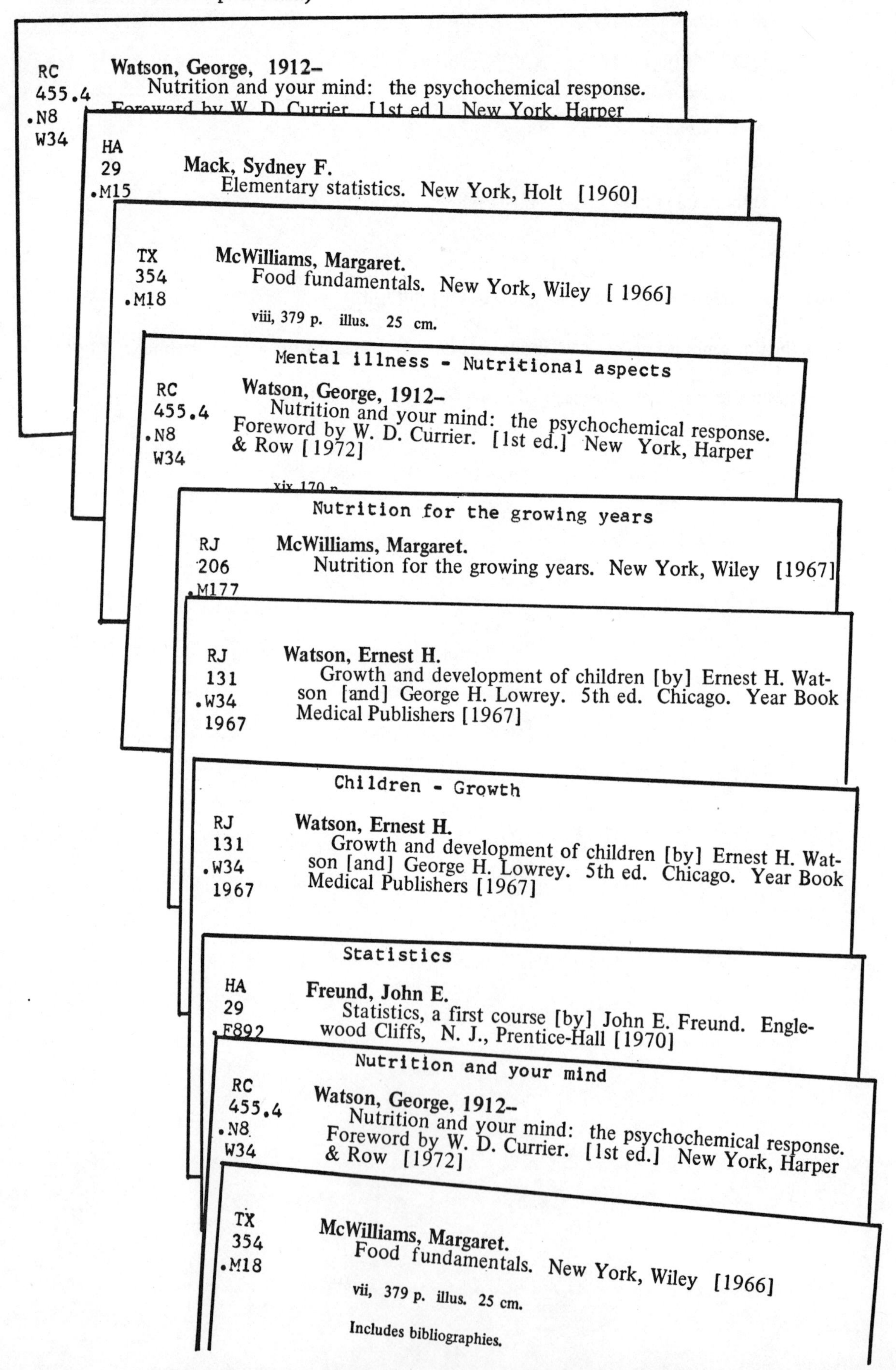

RC 455.4 .N8 W34
Watson, George, 1912–
Nutrition and your mind: the psychochemical response. Foreward by W. D. Currier. [1st ed.] New York, Harper

HA 29 .M15
Mack, Sydney F.
Elementary statistics. New York, Holt [1960]

TX 354 .M18
McWilliams, Margaret.
Food fundamentals. New York, Wiley [1966]
viii, 379 p. illus. 25 cm.

Mental illness - Nutritional aspects
RC 455.4 .N8 W34
Watson, George, 1912–
Nutrition and your mind: the psychochemical response. Foreword by W. D. Currier. [1st ed.] New York, Harper & Row [1972]
xix, 170 p.

Nutrition for the growing years
RJ 206 .M177
McWilliams, Margaret.
Nutrition for the growing years. New York, Wiley [1967]

RJ 131 .W34 1967
Watson, Ernest H.
Growth and development of children [by] Ernest H. Watson [and] George H. Lowrey. 5th ed. Chicago. Year Book Medical Publishers [1967]

Children - Growth
RJ 131 .W34 1967
Watson, Ernest H.
Growth and development of children [by] Ernest H. Watson [and] George H. Lowrey. 5th ed. Chicago. Year Book Medical Publishers [1967]

Statistics
HA 29 .F892
Freund, John E.
Statistics, a first course [by] John E. Freund. Englewood Cliffs, N. J., Prentice-Hall [1970]

Nutrition and your mind
RC 455.4 .N8 W34
Watson, George, 1912–
Nutrition and your mind: the psychochemical response. Foreword by W. D. Currier. [1st ed.] New York, Harper & Row [1972]

TX 354 .M18
McWilliams, Margaret.
Food fundamentals. New York, Wiley [1966]
vii, 379 p. illus. 25 cm.
Includes bibliographies.

1. Give the title of a book by Margaret McWilliams.

____.

2. Give the titles of two books about statistics.

______________________ and ______________________.

3. There are cards for two books by Margaret McWilliams. Who published them? Where? Which was published first?

____

____

____.

4. Look carefully at the cards. How many author cards are there?

____.

5. How many title cards are there? ______________________.

6. How many subject cards are there? What are the subjects?

____

____.

7. There are two authors called Watson. Which will come first in the card catalog?

____.

8. Margaret McWilliams wrote two books. Which will come first in the card catalog?

____.

9. There are ten cards, but there are fewer than ten authors. Alphabetize the authors' names.

____

____

____

____

____.

10. Look at the call numbers. Where in the stacks can you find books about statistics? How do you know?

____.

Exercise 5: Oral Practice

Practice these patterns orally.

A. There *is* a turnstile *in front of* the door.

There *are* hundreds of cards *in* the card catalog.

Use the appropriate verb and the appropriate preposition.

There ______________ many students ______________ the library today.

There ______________ a copy machine ______________ the corner.

There ______________ two signs ______________ the wall.

There ______________ always a librarian ______________ the reference desk.

There ______________ check-out slips ______________ the counter.

There ______________ a carpet ______________ the floor.

There ______________ a desk parallel ______________ the wall.

There ______________ easy chairs ______________ the right ______________ the door.

B. The student went to the library in order to get a book.

to get	a book.
for	a book.

Use the three above patterns for the following. Make three sentences for each.

barber shop	a haircut
doctor's office	a check-up
book store	a textbook
bank	some money
post office	an airmail stamp
police station	a driver's license
hospital	an X-ray

C. 1. Practice the following pattern. Repeat the sentences after your teacher.

The chairs are *so* comfortable *that* the students fall asleep.

The library is *so* quiet *that* the students fall asleep.

The carpet is *so* thick *that* the library isn't noisy.

The library is *so* busy *that* it is always crowded.

The student was *so* critical *that* he complained about the rules to the head librarian.

2. Complete the following sentences.

The student was so lazy that ______________________________.

The chairs were so hard that ______________________________.

The students are so eager that ______________________________.

The shelves are so colorful that ______________________________.

The fines are so expensive that ______________________________.

D. Practice these patterns.

The student looked up a book in the card catalog.

He looked it up.

The student looked for a book in the stacks.

He looked for it.

The student looked at the magazines.

He looked at them.

The student checked out two books.

He checked them out.

Exercise 6: Alphabetical Order

The cards in the card catalog are in drawers in alphabetical order. Students must know the alphabet very well in order to use the catalog efficiently.

A. 1. Look at the following list. The list includes authors, titles, and subjects. Indicate which is a title, an author, or a subject. Titles are italicized.

Example: Helen Keller ______*author*______

The Foster Child ____________

John C. Foster ____________

Whales ____________

Helen Keller's Education ____________

Finland ____________

The deaf ____________

Deaf Children and Disease ____________

Dilmar, Dorothy K. ____________

Finishing Furniture ____________

Francis R. Dillworth ____________

2. Arrange the list in alphabetical order.

____

____

____

____

____

____

____

____

____

____

B. Jim is a busy student. He needs a lot of books, but he doesn't want to waste time. He has a list of things he wants for several classes. Here is his list.

1. A book by an author called William C. Jones about chemistry
2. A book called *The Johnson Administration*
3. A book by Joseph R. Williams called *Accounting Made Easy*
4. A book about early American folksongs for a term paper
5. *Understanding Economics* by Phyllis R. McDuff

Punctuation Rule: Underline the titles of books and periodicals when you write. This is the equivalent of using italics. The titles of books and periodicals are always italicized in print.

Which book should he look for first? second? third? fourth? fifth? What letter of the alphabet should he look under?

Arrange his list in alphabetical order so that he won't waste time.

____

____

____

____

____

Compare your answer with other students' answers. Is there more than one correct answer?

Conversation Practice

A. Two new students are standing in line in front of the circulation desk on the first day of classes.

Librarian: Can I help you?

Student #1: I want to check out this book. How long can I keep it out?

Librarian: For three weeks. Please fill out a check-out slip. After three weeks, we charge 25¢ a day.

Student #2: Can we check out any book we want?

Librarian: You can take out most periodicals and books for three weeks. You can't check out reference books, like encyclopedias. Also there are some books on reserve. Reserve books are set aside for special classes, and students must use them here in the library. You can ask for them here at the desk.

Student #1: Here's the check-out slip.

Librarian: Thank you. The due date is in the back of the book.

Student #1: I'll bring it back in time. Twenty-five cents a day is a lot of money.

Student #2: The library must get rich.

B. A student is standing in front of the circulation desk in the library. He is very impatient. He is tapping his fingers on the desk. He looks irritable.

Librarian: Can I help you?

Student: I need this magazine. (He shows the librarian a piece of paper.) It's not over there on the shelves. I can't find it. I need it right away because I have a test today.

Librarian: What issue do you need?

Student: Issue? I don't understand.

Librarian: What date do you need?

Student: May, 1972.

Librarian: This is a bound periodical. You will find it in the stacks. Did you look up the call number?

Student: I don't understand. I thought the magazines were all over there beside the easy chairs.

Librarian: Those are the recent magazines. Every year we take all the old magazines and bind them together like a book. Then they go on the shelves in the stacks. They are called bound periodicals.

Student: How can I find the call number?

Librarian: Let me show you how to look it up in the card catalog.

Writing

Exercise 1: Writing Sentences—Spatial Relationships

Look at this diagram of the library. Use the diagram and information from the story to complete the sentences. Think about *where* the items are in the library.

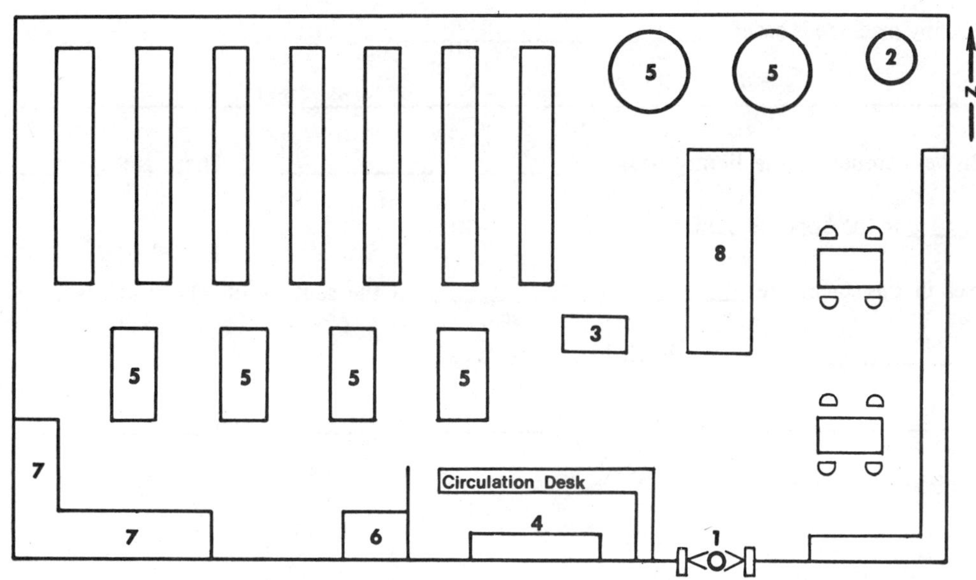

1. turnstile
2. newspapers on racks
3. reference desk
4. reserve books
5. study table
6. photocopy machine
7. tape recorders, etc.
8. card catalog

1. The library door is on the ______________________ wall.

2. The reserve books are on the ______________________ wall behind the ______________________ .

3. There are eight comfortable chairs to the right of the ______________________, near the ____________ .

4. The circulation desk is close to ______________________.

5. The ______________________ is immediately in front of the turnstile.

6. There is one study area with four tables beside ______________________, and there is another study area with ______________________ between ______________________ and ______________________ near ______________________. The former has rectangular tables, but the latter has ____________ ones.

7. The current periodicals are on shelves on the ______________________ wall near ________________ .

8. The stacks are parallel to the ______________________.

9. The card catalog is ______________________ to the east wall and perpendicular to the ______________ wall.

10. The ______________________ is perpendicular to the card catalog.

11. There are two easy chairs on either side of ________________________________ near the magazines.

12. The photocopy machine is beside ______________________.

13. There are ______________________, ______________________, and ______________________ in the south west corner of the library near the ______________________. There are ______________________ in the opposite corner.

14. The shelves in the stacks are ______________________ to the south wall. The students can walk in the aisles ______________________ the shelves in the stacks.

15. The ______________________ is between ______________________ and ______________________ facing the circulation desk.

Exercise 2: Writing about Information—Generalization and Chronological Order

Look at the check-out slip information below.

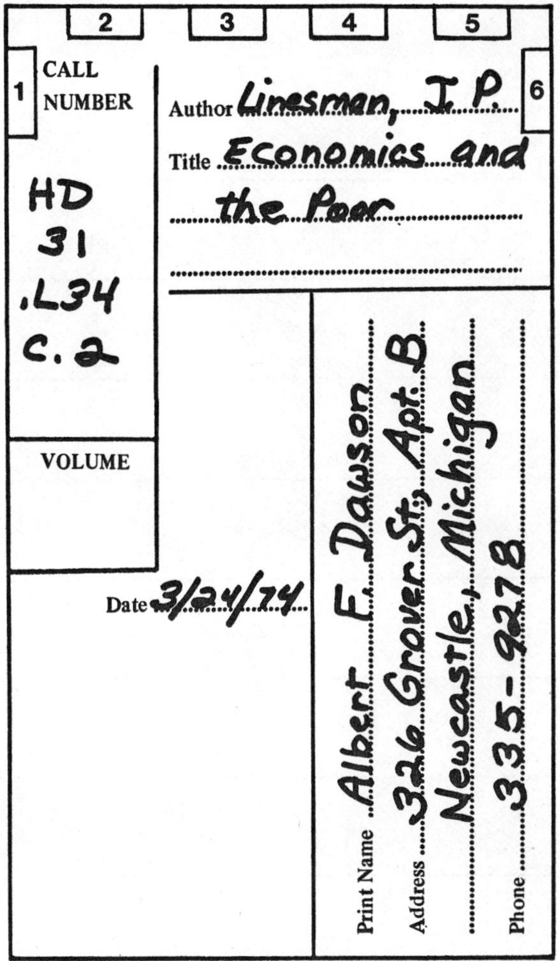

2 | 3 | 4 | 5

1 | CALL NUMBER: HD 31 .L34 c.2

Author: Linesman, J. P. | 6

Title: Economics and the Poor

VOLUME

Date: 3/24/74

Print Name: Albert E. Dawson

Address: 326 Grover St., Apt. B, Newcastle, Michigan

Phone: 335-9278

The student—

1. looked in the card catalog in the drawer J–Le.
2. checked out a book at 10 a.m.
3. entered the library at 9:30 a.m.
4. didn't find the correct card.
5. needed a book by Johnson P. Linesman about economics.
6. filled out a check-out slip.
7. looked in the card catalog under E–Fa.
8. found so many cards that he was confused.
9. looked in the next card catalog drawer and found the correct card.
10. wrote down the call number.

11. located two copies of the book next to each other.
12. went to the stacks.
13. walked back to the circulation desk.
14. left through the turnstile.

A. Put the information in chronological order. Make a list.

B. Make some inferences about the student. What kind of a student is he? Discuss your ideas with your classmates.

C. Write a composition about him. Look at the check-out slip for his name, etc.

1. Start with general information:

his name	his occupation
his address	your generalization (inference) about him

2. Describe his visit to the library. Use chronological order. Use information from the story and from the diagram of the library.

D. Reread your composition. Does your description of his visit prove your inference? Is your inference relevant?

Exercise 3: Writing Classification

A. The card catalog has three kinds of cards. It has author cards, title cards, and subject cards.

When we divide things into groups, we are classifying. We are making a classification.

1. The library has a lot of different things.

   Divide the following into groups making a classification.

   chairs

   videotape machines

   periodicals

   tables

   tapes

   tape recorders

   carpet

   microfilm reader

   desks

   books

   How many groups did you make? What are they?

2. Is there only one way to classify these things?

   How many ways can you think of? Share your ideas with your classmates.

B. One librarian divides the students in the library into two groups, good and bad students. This is a very simple classification.

1. Make a list of characteristics for each group.

   Example:

   Good students always write down the correct call number.

   Bad students smoke in the library.

Good Students	*Bad Students*
____________________	____________________
____________________	____________________
____________________	____________________
____________________	____________________
____________________	____________________

2. Which sentences are good classifications for the beginning of a paragraph about students in the library? Discuss.

   a. The former are noisy.

   b. They always fill out the check-out slips accurately.

   c. The library has two kinds of customers.

   d. We can divide college students in the library into two groups according to their behavior.

   e. The second group never returns books on time.

3. When can we use *the former* and *the latter?*

C. "Students come to the library for different reasons," the librarian said. "Some come in order to find information. Others come in order to study, and the other group comes to relax and sleep in the comfortable chairs."

This librarian divides students into three groups. He *classifies* the students in the library.

1. Complete the following paragraphs.

   There are usually three ____________ of students in the library, according to the librarian. The first kind is ____________ for information. He uses ____________ and ____________. He looks up ____________ in the ____________. Sometimes he asks ____________ questions. He usually ____________ out a lot of ____________.

   The second kind of student comes in order to ____________. He brings ____________ with him and sits in the ____________ area at one of the ____________. He is usually quiet. He seldom asks ____________ or ____________ up ____________.

   The third kind is sometimes a nuisance. He comes to ____________. He ____________ with his friends. He always sits ____________. Occasionally, he ____________ and snores.

2. Look at the above paragraphs. The three paragraphs make a composition of classification. What words tell you this is a classification?

3. Why didn't the writer use *former, latter,* and *both?*

4. Write a paragraph of classification about librarians.

____

____

____

____

____

____

____

____

____

____

____

____

____

Classification

General statements:

We can divide __________ into __________ groups.
kinds.
classes.
types.

There are __________ kinds of __________.

__________ has __________ different __________.

Examples:

former	first
latter	second
both	third, etc.
neither	all three, etc.
the one	the one
the other	the others
	other ______
	another

Exercise 4: Using a Colon for Lists

Writers sometimes want to give their readers lists of information. A colon (:) is useful for lists. It is especially useful for writing classification. The list can be long or short.

A. Look at the following sentences.

1. Libraries have two kinds of periodicals: bound periodicals and current periodicals.
2. The University has many specialized library collections: medical, dental, engineering, public health, nursing, law, music, etc.
3. There are many kinds of reference books in the main library: encyclopedias, maps, statistical tables, bibliographies, and so on.
4. Cards in the card catalog are arranged by: author, title, and subject.

What is the rule for using a colon for a list?

B. Punctuate the following sentences.

1. the library has many machines tape recorders microfilm readers videotape machines etc

___

___

2. the college library is divided into several areas the reference area the circulation desk the card catalog the stacks the section for current periodicals and so on

___

___

___

___

3. the local public library has many different collections books for children records pictures books with big print for the elderly books for teenagers tapes for the blind pamphlets about local organizations books of current interest etc

___

___

___

___

4. a college library check-out slip asks for the following information call number author title borrower's name address and phone number

____

____

____

____

Exercise 5: Writing Paragraphs—Classification

A. Read the following information.

Library Vocabulary

Periodical:	A magazine or journal that is published regularly. Sometimes they are called serials or serial publications because they come out in a series. Each periodical has a call number.
Quarterly:	A periodical which comes out four times a year.
Annual:	A periodical which comes out once a year.
Monthly:	A periodical which comes out every month.
Weekly:	A periodical which comes out every week.
Current periodical:	Recent issues of a magazine or journal. Each magazine has a call number.
Bound periodical:	Magazines more than one year old. They are bound together like a book. They have call numbers. You find them in the stacks like books.

B. Complete the following paragraph of classification.

Librarians divide serial publications into two kinds: ______________ and ______________ . The former are ______________, and the latter are ______________ . The ______________ magazines look like ______________ and are on shelves in ______________ . ______________ are displayed on special shelves. Both kinds have ______________ .

C. Complete the following paragraph of classification.

There are ______________________ common kinds of ______________________ according to how often they ____. The ______________________ yearly. The ____ The ________________ weekly, and the ______________________ every month. All of them have ______________________. Students can look up ______________________ in the card catalog.

Exercise 6: Writing Compositions—Classification and Description

Look at the diagram of the library. How many study areas does it have? Write a composition about the study areas.

Describe each area. Give the location of each area in the library.

Use spatial expressions from this unit.

Your composition will be classification and description.

Start with a classification.

The college library has ____________ study areas.

or

There are ____________ study areas in the college library.

Vocabulary for two areas:	Vocabulary for more than two areas:
the former the latter	the first the second the third, etc.
both one the other	all three another the others

____

____

____

____

____

____

____

____

____

____

Extra Vocabulary and Writing Practice

Exercise 1: Vocabulary Review

Match the vocabulary with the appropriate explanation.

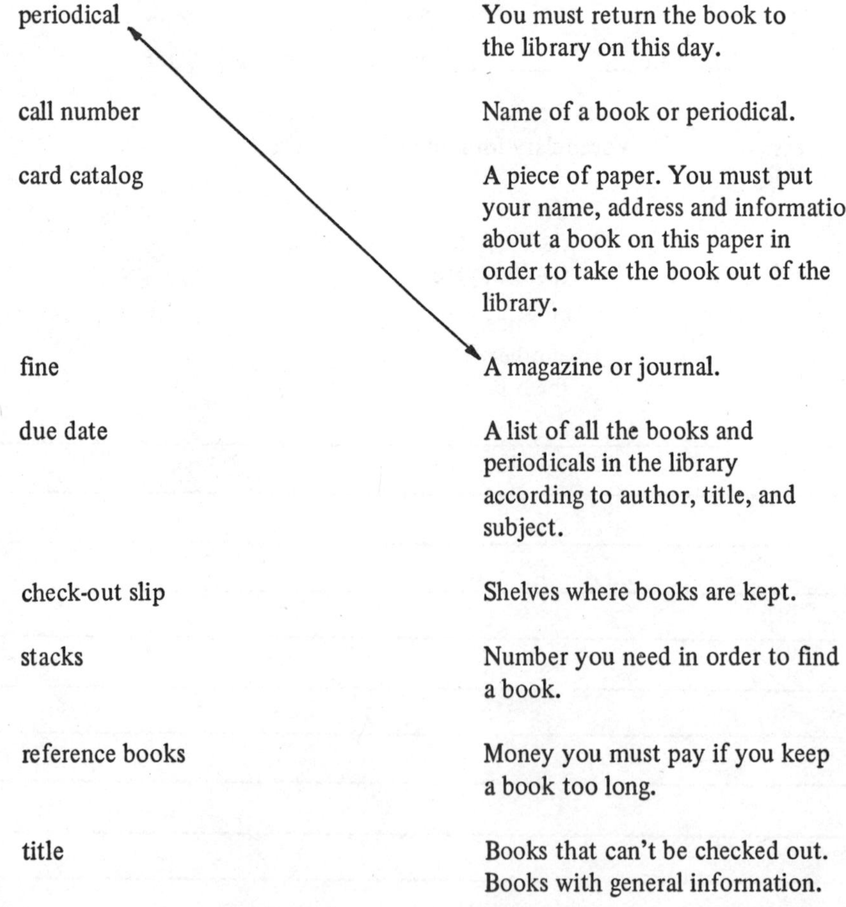

periodical	You must return the book to the library on this day.
call number	Name of a book or periodical.
card catalog	A piece of paper. You must put your name, address and information about a book on this paper in order to take the book out of the library.
fine	A magazine or journal.
due date	A list of all the books and periodicals in the library according to author, title, and subject.
check-out slip	Shelves where books are kept.
stacks	Number you need in order to find a book.
reference books	Money you must pay if you keep a book too long.
title	Books that can't be checked out. Books with general information.

Exercise 2: Vocabulary and Spelling Review

Complete the following sentences.

1. Some students are ____ical of the ___rary rules because they for___ smok___, ___ing, and _____ing inside the ______y.

2. The cards in the c___ c__a__g are in __pha_____al ___er ac____ing to t____, ____or, and sub____.

3. You need the cor____ c___ ____er in order to find a ___k in the s____s.

4. Stu_____ can't __e__ out re_____ books or re_______ books, like en__clo______.

5. The stacks are par___el shel___ of books and b____ per___i___s.

Exercise 3: Compositions

A. Look at the map of the town in Unit 2. The map shows two areas: the park for recreation and the business district. Write a short composition about the two areas. Use vocabulary of spatial relationships. Start with a sentence of classification about the main areas.

B. Look at the following diagram of a typical single room in a college dormitory.

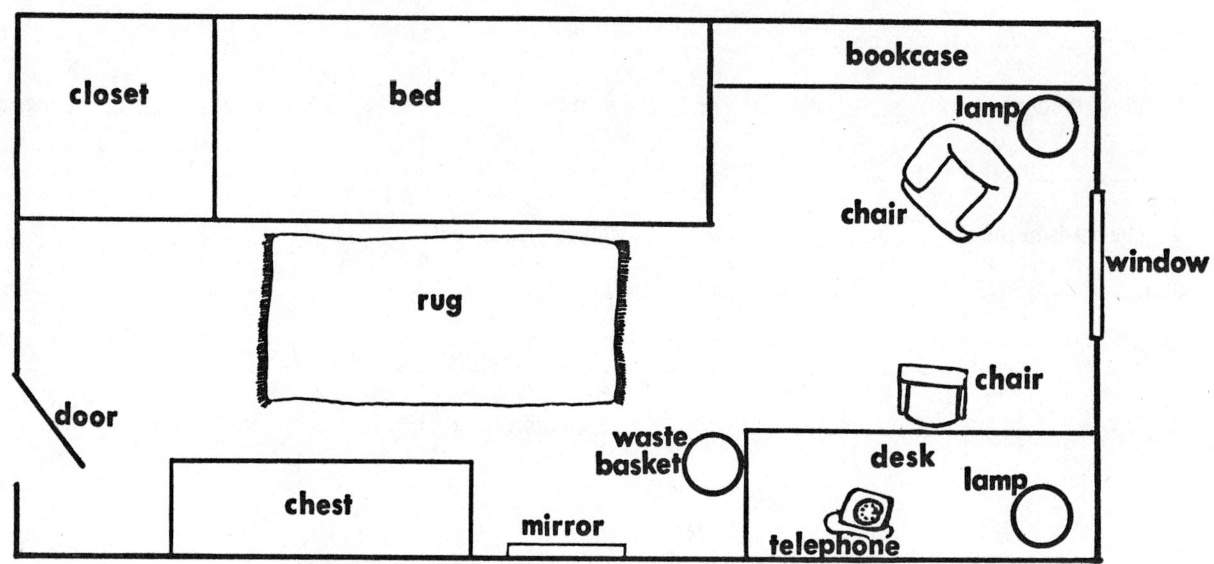

1. Write a paragraph describing this typical dormitory room.

2a. Write a paragraph about your room at school or at home. Draw a diagram first. Use vocabulary of spatial relationships in your description. Start your paragraph with a general statement about the room. Is it attractive? Is it comfortable? Do you like it?

b. Read your paragraph aloud to the class. Do not show the class your diagram. Ask one member of the class to draw a diagram of your room on the blackboard. Check your diagram and the diagram on the board. Was your description accurate enough? What kinds of words can make your description so clear that another person can draw an accurate diagram of your room?

3. Visit the library of your school or town. Write a composition describing the library. You may want to draw a diagram first. Start your composition with a generalization about the library.

4. Describe a typical classroom at your school.

5. Most stores and supermarkets have separate areas for different things. For example, grocery stores usually have an area for meat, an area for milk and milk products, and an area for fruit and vegetables, etc. Clothing stores often have a shoe department, a department for women's clothes, one for men's clothes, and one for children's.

Write a composition describing a store. You may want to visit the store first.

How many departments or areas does the store have?

Make a list of the areas.

Make a list of the kinds of things in each area.

Draw a diagram of the store.

Start your composition with a sentence of classification. Then describe each department. Use vocabulary of spatial relationships. Give examples of the merchandise in each department.

Unit 4: Reading

A Miracle

According to advertisements, certain products can produce miracles. Consider what happened to Mr. William Wilson, for example. For years, Will, as his mother calls him, was the most unpopular man in his firm. Nobody ever invited him home for dinner. Nobody even sent him a Christmas card except his great-aunt Agatha. In the company cafeteria he was never asked to join the other salesmen who laughed loudly and told jokes. Even his secretary seemed to avoid him. She spoke to him as little as possible: "Yes, Sir," "No, Sir," and "A call for you on line three" was the extent of their communication.

Last month, however, everything changed. About the time that great-aunt Agatha died, Will bought a bottle of after-shave lotion. It was fairly expensive, but with the half a million dollars his great-aunt left him in her will, he could afford it. After that, his life changed. Today he is like a new man. The secretaries in the main office smile and wave at him. He never sits alone in the cafeteria; in fact, he is usually surrounded by women.

The advertisement for Will's after-shave lotion says

> Try Miracle
>
> It's guaranteed to change your life

It certainly changed Will's life. Maybe you should try it. It might change yours.

Exercise 1: Reading for Information

A. Read the following sentences. Indicate if the sentence is true or false according to the story. Be prepared to explain your answer.

Example:

Will didn't use any kind of after-shave lotion before last month.

________________	________________	*The story gives too little information for me to decide.*
True	False	Insufficient data

1. Will got money from an elderly male relative.

   ______ True ______ False ______ Insufficient data

2. Will is a salesman.

   ______ True ______ False ______ Insufficient data

3. Will's secretary is usually talkative at the office.

   ______ True ______ False ______ Insufficient data

4. The lotion changed Will's life, and it can change yours too, according to his mother.

   ______ True ______ False ______ Insufficient data

5. The lotion made Will so attractive that he became wealthy and popular.

   ______ True ______ False ______ Insufficient data

6. His great-aunt's name was Agatha Wilson.

   ______ True ______ False ______ Insufficient data

B. Write two sentences about the story. Your sentences must be false according to the author.

   1. ______

   2. ______

C. Write two sentences about the story. Your sentences must be true according to Will's secretary.

   1. ______

   2. ______

Exercise 2: Making Inferences

A. 1. What kind of person is William Wilson?

Which words would you use to describe him?

intelligent	naive	boring
trusting	elderly	suspicious
vain	stupid	fortunate

2. Write two generalizations about him.

a. ____.

b. ____.

B. Complete the following inferences.

1. I think he must be ____________ because he believes in ____________.
2. I think he must be ____________ because ____________.
3. I think he is popular now because ____________.
4. In my opinion, his new friends will ____________.
5. He might ____________.
6. I think he should ____________ because ____________.
7. In my opinion, his mother will probably ____________.
8. Now he can ____________, but he won't because ____________.
9. He is too ____________ to ____________.
10. He wasn't ____________ enough to ____________.

C. 1. In your opinion, what kind of person wrote the story? Discuss your opinions with your classmates.

2. Does the writer believe in advertising?
3. Does the writer think Will is stupid or intelligent?
4. Did the after-shave lotion make Will popular according to the writer?
5. Why did the author write a story about Will?

Exercise 3: Chronological Order and Cause and Result

A. Complete the following sentences.

1. Formerly, Mr. Wilson was ____________________, but now ____________________.
2. Formerly, Mr. Wilson's secretary ____________________, but now ____________________.
3. Prior to last month, Mr. Wilson ____________________, but now ____________________.
4. Prior to his aunt's death, Will ____________________, but now ____________________.
5. Mr. Wilson bought ____________________, and subsequently, ____________________.
6. Mr. Wilson inherited ____________________, and subsequently, ____________________.

B. Match the chronological words that have the *same* meaning.

subsequently	before now
prior to ______	final
formerly	afterward
last	before ______

C. Mr. Wilson became popular after he bought some after-shave lotion. Did he become popular *because* he bought the lotion? Chronological order is concerned with *when* events happen. Cause and result are concerned with *why* events happen.

First / Second } in time *can* be { Cause / Result

Are { First / Second } in time *always* { Cause / Result } ?

Complete the following sentences. Use *before, after,* or *because.* Can some sentences have more than one answer? Why?

1. Mr. Wilson became popular ____________________ he bought the lotion.
2. The secretaries liked Mr. Wilson ____________________ he inherited a lot of money.
3. The secretaries ignored Mr. Wilson ____________________ he was boring.
4. Mr. Wilson became rich ____________________ his great-aunt died.
5. Mr. Wilson was unpopular ____________________ he bought the lotion.

Exercise 4: Oral Practice

Practice these patterns orally.

A. I was late because my watch was slow.

early fast.

Complete the following.

He fell asleep because __________ tired.

She cried because __________ unhappy.

They went to bed because __________ sleepy.

I went __________ because __________ sick.

He dropped the cup because __________ clumsy.

__________ expensive watch because __________ rich.

__________ dropped the box because __________ heavy.

My boss swore because __________ angry.

____________________ because the lecture was boring.

The poor man bought some rice because __________ cheap.

B. My watch was slow, so I was late.
My watch was fast, so I was early.

I felt hungry, so I ate my lunch.
I was thirsty, so I drank some water.

Use your imagination to complete the following.

______________________________ tired, so he ______________________________.

______________________________ unhappy, so she ______________________________.

______________________________ sleepy, so they ______________________________

______________________________ sick, so I ______________________________.

______________________________ clumsy, so he ______________________________

______________________________ rich, so she ______________________________

______________________________ too heavy, so the small boy ______________________________.

______________________________ angry, so he ______________________________.

______________________ cheap, so the poor man ______________________ .

______________________ boring, so ______________________ .

Now change the sentences with *so* to sentences with *because.* First, your teacher or a student will give one form. Then, you respond quickly with the other.

C. Practice these patterns. Repeat the patterns after your teacher.

The lawyer gave the money to Will.
The lawyer gave him the money.

The bank loaned some money to Will.
him some money.

The man bought a gift for his girl friend.
her a gift.

The salesman sold some merchandise to the customer.
him some merchandise.

The patterns below have only *one* correct form.

The bank charged me five percent interest.
The sale saved me ten dollars.
The gift cost me too much money.

D. Make questions with *who* for the following patterns. Use the past tense.

Examples:

Who gave Will the money?

Who(m) did Agatha give the money to?

---

1. buy the lotion

Who ______________________ ?

Who(m) ______________________ for?

2. describe the cafeteria

Who ______________________ ?

Who(m) ______________________ to?

3. inherit the money

Who ____?

Who(m) ____ from?

4. explain the problem

Who ____?

Who(m) ____ to?

5. get the invitation

Who ____?

Who(m) ____ from?

6. do the work

Who ____?

Who(m) ____ for?

7. type a letter

Who ____?

Who(m) ____ to?

Who(m) ____ for?

8. answer the question

Who ____?

Who(m) ____ for?

9. lend some money

Who ____?

Who(m) ____ to?

10. borrow some money

Who ____?

Who(m) ____ from?

Exercise 5: Cause and Result

The following sentence patterns are used for cause and result.

– – – – , so – – – – .
– – – – ; therefore, – – –.
– – – – because – – – – .
– – – – because of (noun).
– – – – so ______ that – – – .
– – – – – make ______ ______.

cause ↓ ____________, so ____________ ↓ result.

cause ↓ ____________; therefore, ____________ ↓ result.

result ↓ ____________ because ____________ ↓ cause.

result ↓ ____________ because of ____________ ↓ cause.

____________ so ____________ ↓ cause that ____________ ↓ result.

cause ↓ ____________ makes ____________ ____________ ↓ result.

A. 1. Which usually comes first in time—the cause or the result?

2. Look at the following pairs of events. Which is the cause? Which is the result?

a. The salesman ate ten sandwiches. ____________________

The salesman felt sick. ____________________

b. Mr. Streeter feels unhappy. ____________________

Mr. Streeter lost his pet dog. ____________________

c. I took my umbrella to work. ____________________

It was raining yesterday. ____________________

d. The secretary was incompetent. ____________________

The manager fired the secretary. ____________________

e. The tenant on the first floor complained about the noise. ____________________

The tenant in the basement turned up his radio. ____________________

B Look at the above pairs of sentences. Write a sentence of cause and result about each pair of sentences. Substitute pronouns in appropriate places.

Example: The manager fired the secretary because she was incompetent.

---

1. ______________________________, so ______________________________ .
2. ______________________________; therefore, ______________________________ .
3. ______________________________ because ______________________________ .
4. ______________________________, so ______________________________ .
5. ______________________________; therefore, ______________________________ .

C. Use the pattern *because of* (noun) for this pair.

{ Mr. Streeter feels unhappy. }
{ Mr. Streeter lost his pet dog. }

Change one of the sentences to fit the pattern.

____________________ because of ____________________.

D. Use the pattern *so* ________ *that* ________ for this pair.

{ The secretary was incompetent. }
{ The manager fired the secretary. }

____.

E. Use the pattern ________ *make* (person) (adjective) for this pair.

{ The salesman ate ten sandwiches. }
{ The salesman felt sick. }

Change the sentences to fit the pattern.

____________________ made ____________________ ____________________.

F. Change this pair to fit the pattern *so* ____________________ *that* ____________________.

{ The salesman ate ten sandwiches. }
{ The salesman felt sick. }

____________________ so ____________________ that ____________________

Exercise 6: Logical Questions

A. Write appropriate questions for the following answers.

	Question	*Short Answer*
1.	____________________?	His great-aunt.
2.	____________________?	In order to buy some after-shave lotion.
3.	____________________?	Because he was unpopular.
4.	____________________?	The other salesmen.
5.	____________________?	Because of his inheritance.

B. We often know the kind of answer we want to get. For example, we want to learn a date, or a person's name.

1. Match the question pattern with the appropriate kind of answer.

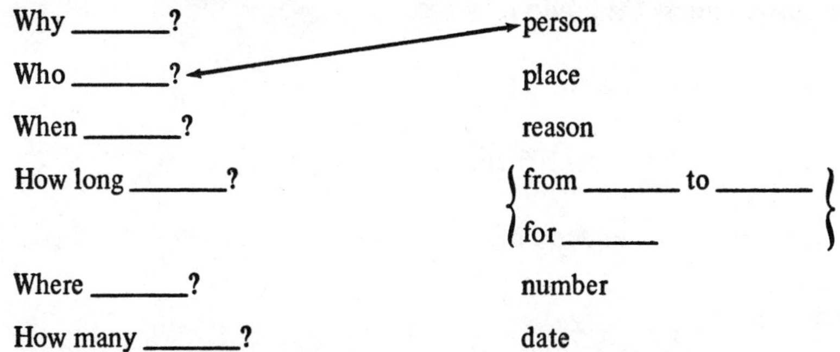

2. Write appropriate questions about the story for the following kinds of answers.

Example:

Why did Will inherit a lot of money? reason

	Question	*Kind of Answer*
a.	____________________?	date
b.	____________________?	person
c.	____________________?	from *date* to *date*
d.	____________________?	an amount of money
e.	____________________?	reason

Conversation Practice

Will is at his aunt's lawyer's office. He and the lawyer are discussing his aunt's will and his inheritance.

Lawyer: Do you have your own lawyer, Mr. Wilson?

Will: No, I never needed a lawyer before now. Maybe you can help me.

Lawyer: I'll be glad to advise you.

Will: When do I get my money?

Lawyer: The money will be transferred to your bank, but we have some other matters to discuss first.

Will: Send it to National City Bank. Last month I tried to get a loan there for a used car. I only wanted $200, but they turned me down. I am really going to enjoy going there now. I'm a wealthy man now. I guess I'll buy a new car.

Lawyer: We should discuss taxes first, Mr. Wilson.

Will: I don't owe any. My boss takes them out of my pay check.

Lawyer: I'm afraid you don't understand. As your aunt's heir, you must pay inheritance taxes.

Will: How much?

Lawyer: I can make an estimate today; later I can give you an accurate calculation.

Will: OK. How much is your estimate?

Lawyer: You will probably pay 45 percent on the first $300,000 and 60 percent on the remainder.

Will: That's not a tax, that's a robbery. Let's see, for 45 percent of $300,000.00 we multiply by forty-five. I figure one hundred and thirty thousand dollars. Can that be right?

Lawyer: I think $135,000 is accurate. Plus $120,000 for the remainder.

Will: You mean the government is going to take $255,000? Subtract that from $500,000. That leaves me only $245,000. I came in here half a millionaire, and I'm going out a poor man again.

Writing

Exercise 1: Writing Sentences

Join each pair of short sentences to form one sentence.

Example:

Mr. Wilson had too few friends.

Mr. Wilson felt lonely.

________________________; therefore, ____________.

Mr. Wilson had too few friends; therefore, he felt lonely.

---

1. Mr. Wilson had too little money.

   Mr. Wilson was very unpopular with the secretaries in the office.

   ____ because

   ____.

2. The man had a lot of expenses.

   The man made a withdrawal from his savings account.

   ____

   because ____________________________________.

3. The lawyer's advice saved the client $15,000.

   The lawyer charged him a large fee.

   ____, so

   ____.

4. His aunt died.

   He became rich.

   Because of ________________________, __________________.

5. His aunt died.

   His aunt donated a large sum of money to charity.

   Prior to ________________, ____________________________

   ____.

6. He bought an electric calculator.

   He figured out his taxes.

   ____ in order to

   ____ .

7. He inherited half a million dollars.

   His aunt was rich.

   ______________________ so ______________________ that

   ____ .

8. The customer asked for a refund.

   The lotion didn't produce a change in the customer's life.

   ____ ,

   so ____ .

9. The extravagant man asked his mother for a loan.

   The gift to his girl friend cost him too much money.

   ____ ;

   therefore, ____ .

10. The bank manager refused the young man's application for a loan.

    The young man spent all his inheritance from his father.

    ____

    because ____ .

Exercise 2: Writing about Information—Cause and Result

A. Will was unpopular before his inheritance. Soon afterward, he became extremely popular.

Write a short paragraph of cause and result about Will's experience. Start with a generalization. Then give examples. Use vocabulary of chronological order, and vocabulary of cause and result.

Becoming rich can make people popular. Consider Will Wilson, for example. Last year, he ______________________________. Nobody ______________________________. But after his aunt's death, he ______________________________, and then ______________________________. They ______________________________ and ______________________________ because ______________________________. Because of ______________________________, he is now ______________________________.

B. Advertisements sometimes make promises.

Look at this ad.

Don't sit at home
every night
waiting for a date.
USE
BRIGHT TEETH
the toothpaste
that
GUARANTEES
KISSES

Complete the following paragraph.

According to this toothpaste ad, ______________________________ will make you ______________________________. Your ______________________________ will be so ______________________________ that you will have lots of ______________________________. You will be so ______________________________ that ______________________________ will ______________________________ you. In my opinion, people should buy ______________________________ in order to ______________________________. People don't have ______________________________

__________ because of ____________________. They have ____________________ because people like them. In fact, I never use ____________________ and I have ____________________ any way.

C. Look at this ad for a children's encyclopedia.

> Does your child
> have
> TROUBLE IN SCHOOL?
> Buy
> *Easy Answers*
> the
> NEW
> ENCYCLOPEDIA
> for
> CHILDREN

Mrs. Johnson's seven year old son, Peter, has a lot of trouble in school. He can't read very well, and he can't spell. He is always hitting the other children and bothering the teacher, according to his report card. Should Mrs. Johnson buy the encyclopedia for her son?

1. According to the ad, children have trouble in school because ____________________

   ____________________.

2. According to Peter's teacher, Mrs. Johnson's son has a lot of trouble in school because __________

   ____________________.

3. According to the encyclopedia company, she should buy him *Easy Answers* because __________

   ____________________.

4. In your opinion, should she buy the encyclopedia? Why or why not? ____________________

   ____________________.

5. Mrs. Johnson bought the encyclopedia, and subsequently, her son learned to read fairly well.

   a. ____________________ because of ____________________, according to the ad.

   b. ____________________, according to his teacher.

6. Mrs. Johnson didn't buy the encyclopedia, and her son didn't learn to read.

____; therefore, ____________________

____, according to the publisher.

____; therefore, ____________________

____, according to the teachers at Peter's school.

7. Mrs. Johnson didn't buy *Easy Answers.* Afterward, her son became a good student at another school.

____ because

____.

Exercise 3: Paragraphs of Advice

Most people like to give advice to others: to their family, to their friends, to their acquaintances, and to their employees. Often people don't follow their friends' advice, but they usually take their employer's advice seriously.

A. Mr. Wilson's secretary is not satisfactory.

Write a short paragraph of advice. Tell her what a good secretary does. Tell her what she should do.

Mr. Wilson is a ______________________ and a businessman. His secretary should __________ __________. A good secretary may ______________________, but she will never __________ __________. You should always ______________________ because ______________________. You can ______________________, or you can ______________________. You ______________ __________, but you shouldn't because it makes ______________________. You can sometimes ______________________, but you should always ______________________ because maybe Mr. Wilson will ______________________.

B. Your father is going to inherit $500,000 next month. Write him a letter of advice. Tell him what he should do with the money.

Use the following vocabulary.

first	buy	borrow	because	should	must
next	give	deposit	because of	might	will
then, etc.	donate	lend	so	can	follow advice

your → ____________________
address → ____________________

date → ____________________

Dear Father,

Love,

____________________ ← your name

Exercise 4: Writing about Money

A. 1. Mr. Wilson inherited half a million dollars from his aunt. He paid inheritance taxes of 45 percent on the first $300,000 and 60 percent on the remaining $200,000.

How much money did he have left after taxes?

______________________________.

2. a. He deposited the rest in the bank at 7 percent interest *per annum*. How much interest will he receive every year?

______________________________.

b. How did you calculate the amount? Did you multiply? divide? add? etc. Explain.

______________________________.

3. He wants to buy an expensive car soon. The kind he likes costs $6,000.00. He can get a loan for the car at 11 percent yearly interest. How much money will he have to pay for interest the first year?

______________________________.

4. Should he take the money from his bank account to pay for the car? Should he borrow money to buy the car? Explain.

____

______________________________.

5. Will calculates that he needs a minimum income of $15,000 a year from his inheritance in order to live well. How much must he keep in his bank account to receive the sum he needs every year?

____

______________________________.

B. Will's secretary wants to borrow a thousand dollars from him because she has a lot of debts. She won't pay any interest. Should Will turn her down? Why?

____

____

____

____

C. You are Will's financial adviser. What should he do with his money? Write a paragraph of advice. In the final sentence tell him why he should follow your advice.

____

____

____

____

____

Exercise 5: Semicolon and Comma

A. Examine the following three examples.

1. Banks pay interest on deposits.   Banks charge interest on loans.
2. Banks pay interest on deposits, and banks charge interest on loans.
3. Banks pay interest on deposits;   banks charge interest on loans.

   1. The first example is a pair of sentences.

      What is the punctuation rule?

   2. The second example is one sentence with a comma (,).

      Give the punctuation rule for

      – – –, and – – –.

   3. The third example is one sentence with a semicolon (;).

      Give the punctuation rule for

      – – –; – – –.

B. Examine the following three examples.

1. The customer borrowed money, so he paid interest.
2. The customer borrowed money. Therefore, he paid interest.
3. The customer borrowed money; therefore, he paid interest.

   1. The first example is one sentence with *so.*

      What is the punctuation rule?

   2. The second example is a pair of sentences.

      What is the punctuation rule?

   3. The third example is one sentence with a semicolon and *therefore.*

      What is the punctuation rule?

   4. There are two punctuation rules for *therefore.*

      What are they?

C. Write the following sentences with correct punctuation.

1. the inheritance tax is very high therefore the heirs paid almost half their inheritance in taxes

___

___

2. advertisements for cosmetics are often misleading so you shouldnt rely on them

___

___

3. he subtracted the wrong amount therefore his calculation was inaccurate

___

___

4. i dont believe in miracles only naive people do

___

___

5. the man had a lot of debts therefore the bank rejected his application for a loan

___

___

Exercise 6: Cause and Result

People often want to buy products for stupid reasons. Look at these ads. According to the ads, why should people purchase these products?

KIDS

TELL MOM

to buy

RAINBOWS

the sugary cereal.

It changes

color

in milk.

Get off the beaten track!

Be your OWN Man.

SMOKE

BRAVES.

The Daring Man's

Tobacco.

Unit 4
Writing

Write a short composition about advertising and why people buy products.

Use these two ads as examples.

1. Start with a question.

   Why do people buy harmful products?

   or

   Why do people buy unnecessary things?

   or

   Why do people waste money?

2. Make a generalization next.

   In my opinion, many people ________________________ because of advertising.

3. Give examples. Use vocabulary for examples.

   For example,

   Consider ____________, for example

   Look at ____________, for example

   Let me give you an example.

4. Use vocabulary like:

because	for	buy	need to
because of	in order to	want	want to
so	change	like	expect to
therefore	make ____ ____	need	believe in

____

____

____

____

____

____

____

____

____

____

Exercise 7: Classification

A. People save money for a lot of reasons. Some people save money because they like expensive clothes; others save money for their children's education, or for their old age.

Why do you save money? Write a short composition about your reasons.

1. Start with a classification.

   I save money for ____________ reasons.

   or

   There are ____________ reasons why I save money.

   or

   Why do I save money? There are ____________ reasons.

2. Explain each reason.

3. Use vocabulary like:

because	in order to	want to (verb)
because of	buy	expect to (verb)
so	need	plan to (verb)
for	want	

____

____

____

____

____

____

____

____

____

____

____

____

____

B. Being wealthy can have a lot of advantages. Being wealthy can also have a lot of disadvantages. Write a short composition about the advantages *or* the disadvantages.

1. Make a list of ideas first. Be sure your ideas are relevant.

2. Start with a generalization which is a classification.

    Being rich has ____________ main disadvantages.

    or

    Being rich has ____________ main advantages.

3. Give examples to prove your generalization.

4. Use vocabulary like:

because	lend	should
because of	give	must
so	ask for	want (person) to (verb)
therefore	popular	expect (person) to (verb)
buy	lonely	persuade (person) to (verb)
want	friendly	tell (person) to (verb)
borrow	can	advise (person) to (verb)

Extra Vocabulary and Writing Practice

Exercise 1: Vocabulary Review

Complete the following sentences. Choose the appropriate words from the list below.

1. According to ______________ authorities, tobacco is ______________, but cigarette manufacturers don't ______________.

danger	medicine	agreement	disagree
dangerous	medical	agree	agreeable

2. Because the secretary __________ her mother a lot of money, she ______________ to the bank for a ______________.

owned	lend	apply
owed	loan	application
borrowed	borrow	applied

3. The bank pays customers __________ on __________, but ______________ must pay the bank interest on ______________.

interest	borrow	lend	deposited
interesting	borrowers	loans	deposits
interested	withdraw	payments	tax

4. The __________ gave his client some good __________ about ______________ taxes.

inheritance	lawyers	legal	advice
heir	lawyer	illegal	method

5. ______________ elderly people are often ______________ with their relatives because of their ______________.

popular	wealthy	generosity
unpopular	wealth	generous

Exercise 2: Vocabulary and Spelling Review

1. You should cal___ate ac___ately the in___est you must pay on a l__n from the ___k.

2. The ab_______tion for "adver____ment" is "ad."

3. T____past_ ads often pro____ wh___ t__th and p__ular___.

4. The gen__ous mill______re don___d a large s_m of money to the p__r.

5. Pr___ to his aunt's ___th, the se_____ar___ av___ed Will, but now he is sur______ed by fr__nds.

Exercise 3: Compositions

A. Write a composition of classification about the reasons people go to college.

1. Start with a generalization.

    People go to college for ____________ main reasons.

    or

    There are ____________ main reasons why people go to college.

    or

    Why do people go to college? There are ____________ main reasons.

2. Explain each reason and give examples.

3. Try to use some of the following vocabulary.

in order to	want to	another
for	plan to	the other
because	expect to	former
because of	some	latter
so	others	second, etc.
therefore	first	

B. Write a composition about *one* of the following generalizations.

Becoming rich can make people generous.

or

Being a good athlete sometimes makes a person famous.

or

Becoming famous doesn't always make a person happy.

or

Working hard doesn't guarantee success.

1. Start with the generalization.
2. Give examples.
3. Use vocabulary of chronological order.
4. Use vocabulary of cause and result.

C. Some people have a lot of friends. Do you have one very popular friend? Write a composition about your friend. Explain why he/she is popular.

D. Look at this advertisement.

Learn to Speak
any
Foreign Language
at home.
Listen to our tapes
only *five minutes* every day.
Easy!
Inexpensive!
Write for our free brochure today.

Your friend, a travel agent, is interested in learning to speak a foreign language. He wants to buy these tapes. Write a letter of advice to your friend. Explain what he should (shouldn't) do. Tell him to follow your advice.

Unit 5: Reading

Home Is Best

Capital City and Smithsville are two fairly large towns in the Midwest near Chicago. Neither is as well known as Chicago, but the inhabitants of both are equally proud of their respective hometowns.

People in Capital City love its quiet narrow tree-lined streets and its many small neighborhood parks. They boast that their hometown has no ugly slums, a low rate of crime, and very little heavy traffic. Because it is the seat of the state legislature, Capital City has many stately old buildings, such as the Lawyers' Club in the park by the lake, and the county museum with its pioneer farm exhibits.

Smithsville, on the other hand, is a bustling, thriving, industrial center. It too has a lake, but unlike that of Capital City, its lake is the center of the city's industrial development. Instead of trees and park benches, Smithsville's lake is surrounded by factories and smoking chimneys. Smithsville is also different from its quieter neighbor in its style of architecture. The tall modern office buildings downtown, the new shopping centers in the suburbs, and the wide crowded streets seem more attractive to Smithsville's residents than the old-fashioned neighborhoods they replaced.

When people from the more rural city return from a visit to Smithsville, they always say, "I'm glad to be home again. That place makes me nervous. It's a fine place to visit, but I wouldn't want to live there." After a visit to Capital City, citizens of Smithsville say exactly the same thing.

Exercise 1: Reading for Explicit and Implicit Information

A. Read the passage about the two cities. Reread the passage quickly to find answers to the following questions.

Indicate if you can find the answer in the passage.

I can find the answer.

or

I can't find the exact answer, but I can make a fairly accurate inference.

or

The passage gives no relevant information.

Be prepared to explain your answers.

1. Which city has higher taxes for police protection?

____

2. What kind of people live in Capital City? What is one of their major occupations?

____

____

3. Which city had the faster growth in population last year?

____

4. Which city has more facilities for recreation?

____

5. Are there any slums in Smithsville?

____

6. Which city has more retired people? industrial workers? policemen? car salesmen?

____

____

7. Which lake has cleaner water?

____

8. Which city has a problem because of air pollution?

____

B. Why is it difficult to answer some of these questions? When a passage gives us definite information, we say the information is *explicit.* When the passage does *not* give us definite information but we can figure it out, we say the information is *implicit.* Look at the above questions again. Which answers are *explicit* in the passage?

C. The passage doesn't give exact information about some of the questions, but we can make a fairly accurate inference. For example, I can infer that the water in Smithsville's lake might be polluted because it is surrounded by factories.

Complete the following.

1. I can make an inference about ______________________________

because ______________________________.

2. I assume that ______________________________

because ______________________________.

D. Sometimes we can't find the information we want because it isn't stated explicitly, and it isn't stated implicitly either. Then we say we have no relevant data (information). Look at the questions again. Are there any questions you can't answer because the passage has no relevant data? What kind of information would you need to answer those questions?

Complete the following.

I need information about ____________________

in order to answer questions about ____________________

____________________.

Exercise 2: Making Inferences

We can make inferences about the opinions of the citizens of the two towns.

Read the following direct quotations.

A. Who might say this? Make an inference.

Example:

"Modern architecture is ugly."

A real estate salesman who lives in Capital City might say this.

---

1. "Smithsville can't ever have too many factories. Jobs are more important than clean air."

____

____

2. "Modern architecture is attractive."

____

____

3 "Maybe you like a lot of quiet open spaces, but cities need factories for taxes."

____

____

4. "Factories pollute the lake, and buses pollute the air. The city should move the factories outside the city limits. Then people can drive to work and find parking places."

____

____

5. "Cities like Capital City are dying. They need industry."

___

___

6. "City growth is good for the farmers because they can sell their land at a profit."

___

___

B. Look at each of the quotations again. Do you agree or disagree with the quotation? Why?

Example:

"Modern architecture is ugly."

I disagree with this idea because I like tall buildings with lots of glass windows and modern design.

1. ___ because
agree/disagree
___ .

2. ___ because
agree/disagree
___ .

3. ___ because
agree/disagree
___ .

4. ___ because
agree/disagree
___ .

5. ___ because
agree/disagree
___ .

6. ___ because
agree/disagree
___ .

Exercise 3: Comparison and Contrast

A. Capital City is like Smithsville because they both have lakes. This is a statement of *comparison.* It compares the two cities.

Reread the passage about the two cities. Find five other pieces of information that are *comparisons.*

Comparison

1. Both ____________________ are near ____________________.

2. Capital City is ____________________, and ____________________ is too.

3. Smithsville isn't ____________________, and ____________________ either. Neither is ____________________.

4. The citizens of each ____________________ are like ____________________ because ____________________ ____________________.

5. The citizens of Capital City are similar to ____________________ because ____________________ ____________________.

B. Capital City is different from Smithsville because the former isn't industrial, but the latter is. This is a statement of *contrast.* It *contrasts* the two cities.

(cóntrast: noun/contrást: verb)

Reread the passage about the two cities. Find five other items of information that are *contrasts.*

Contrast

1. ____________________, but ____________________.

2. ____________________ is different from ____________________ because ____________________.

3. ____________________ is ____________________ than ____________________.

4. ____________________ has fewer ____________________ than ____________________.

5. The lake in Smithsville is not as ____________________ as ____________________. On the contrary, it is polluted.

C. Examine the following sentences. Which are comparison? Which are contrast?

Example:

The industrial city had more traffic than the rural town.	*contrast*

1. Some industries pollute the air, but others don't. ____________
2. Large cities are usually more crowded than small towns. ____________
3. My hometown is different from yours. ____________
4. Both New York and Chicago have skyscrapers. ____________
5. Industrial cities are often less attractive than rural towns to elderly citizens who want to retire in a peaceful place. ____________
6. Bustling cities with heavy traffic and crowded streets can be exciting; on the other hand, they make some people nervous. ____________
7. Smoke from factories is similar to car exhaust because both pollute the air. ____________
8. Air pollution is as dangerous as water pollution. ____________
9. Capital City has a fire department with modern equipment; however, it is much smaller than that of its industrial neighbor. ____________
10. Smithsville has citizens of many nationalities who are all equally proud of their respective homelands. ____________

D. 1. Reread the story about Smithsville and Capital City. Circle the vocabulary of comparison. Underline the vocabulary of contrast.

2. Look at the following list of words and phrases. Divide the list into two groups, the first for comparison and the second for contrast.

however	but	have---in common	different from
similar to	and---either	be like	the same as
less than	both	more than	as---as
respective	on the other hand	and---too	neither
similar	different	on the contrary	be alike

Comparison	*Contrast*
1. ______________________	1. ______________________
2. ______________________	2. ______________________
3. ______________________	3. ______________________
4. ______________________	4. ______________________
5. ______________________	5. ______________________
6. ______________________	6. ______________________
7. ______________________	7. ______________________
8. ______________________	8. ______________________
9. ______________________	
10. ______________________	
11. ______________________	
12. ______________________	

Exercise 4: Reading Graphs and Tables

A. Look at the following graph which is a circle graph. It shows how Capital City spent city taxes in 1970. Look at the graph for information which is explicit and inferences which are implicit.

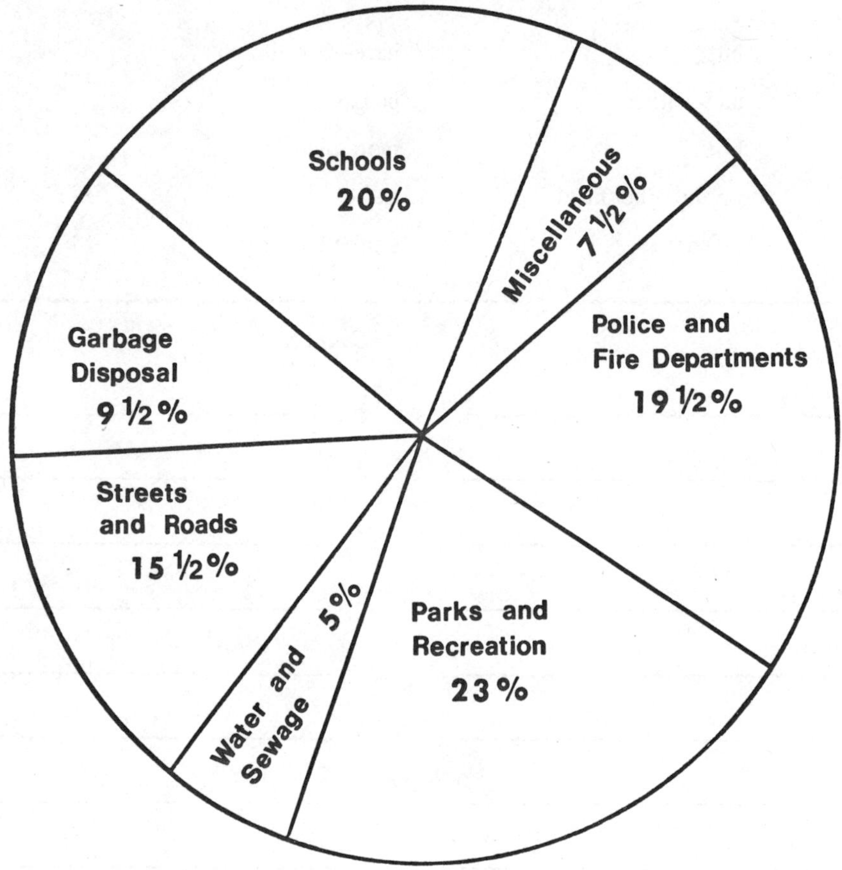

Complete the following sentences.

1. In 1970, Capital City spent a greater percentage of its tax money for ____________________ than for ____________________.

2. ____________________ and ____________________ were almost equally expensive in 1970.

3. ____________________ cost almost as much as ____________________ in ____________________.

4. Citizens who live in Capital City must enjoy ____________________ and ____________________.

5. Schools cost less than ______________________ in 1970 according to ______________________; therefore, there are probably fewer ______________________ than ______________________ in the city.

6. The low crime rate is probably due to the ______________________ share of each tax dollar that ______________________ spends for ______________________.

7. For every tax dollar it spends, Capital City uses ______________________ cents for ______________________.

B. Look at the following graph which is a bar graph. It shows the number of businesses and industries in Smithsville from 1960 to 1970.

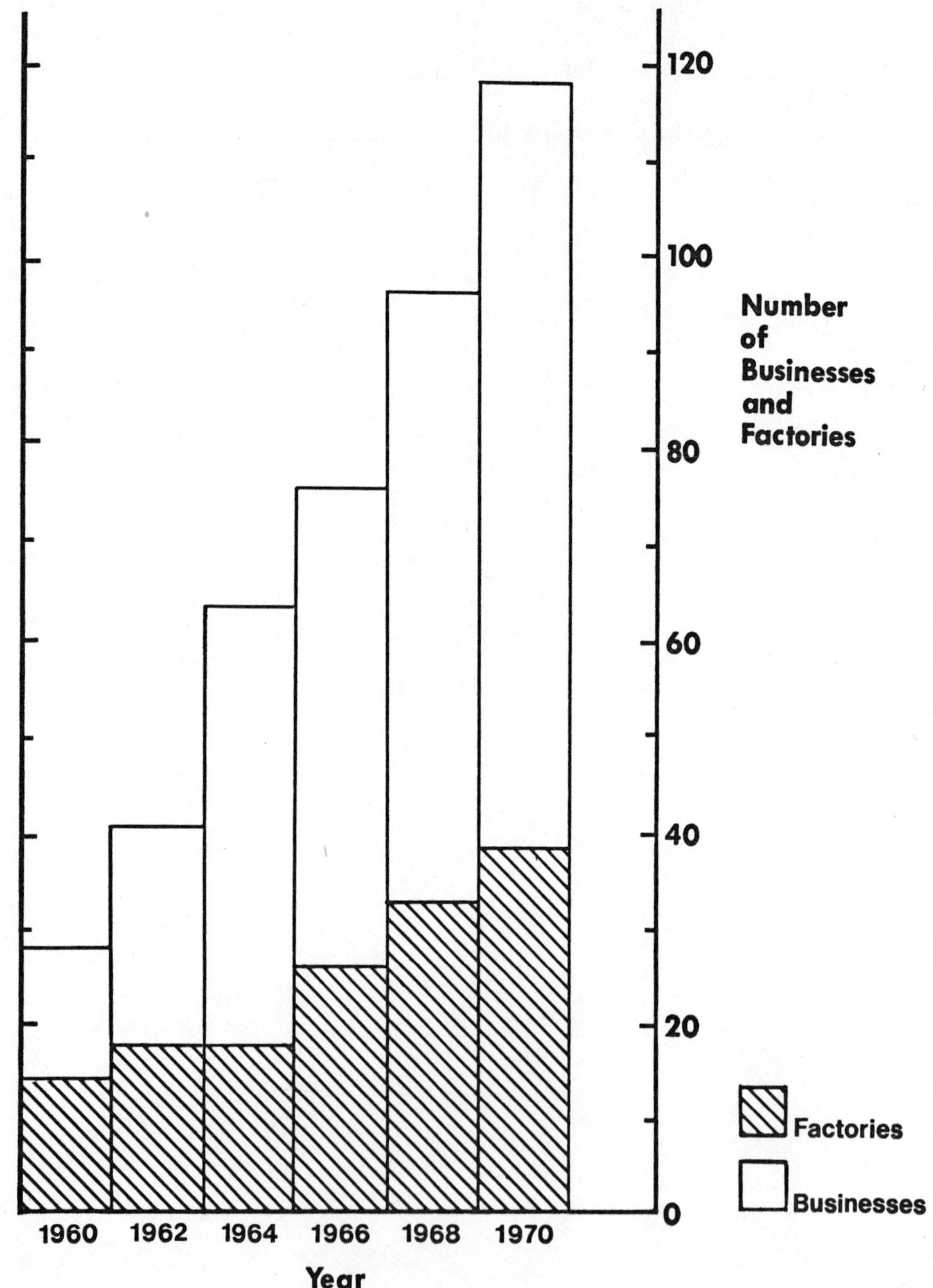

Complete the following sentences.

1. The number of ____________________ increased faster than the number of ____________________ between ____________________ and ____________________.

2. There were ____________________ new factories in ____________________ in ____________________ .

3. The total number of ____________________ and ____________________ rose every year, but ____ .

4. ____________________ didn't decrease between ____________________ and __________, and ____ didn't either.

5. The increase in ____________________ was greater between ____________________ and ____________________ than between ____________________ and ____________________ .

C. Look at the following table which gives the number of major crimes in Smithsville from 1960 to 1970. You may want to *round off* some of the numbers. For example, you can round off 579 to 580, or 603 to 600.

	1960	1962	1964	1966	1968	1970
Murders	7	12	5	15	17	24
Car thefts	1212	1440	1094	1307	1621	2398
Armed robberies	127	132	94	141	150	196
Burglaries	406	483	430	579	603	721

Complete the following sentences.

1. There were twice as many ____________________ in ____________________ as in ______________

2. All major crimes decreased in number in ____________________, but the number of ______________ ___________ decreased by the greatest percentage.

3. After ____________________, the crime rate in Smithsville ____________________ steadily from year to year.

4. The number of ____________________ showed the greatest increase between ____________________ and ____________________.

5. There were almost three times as many ____________________ in ____________________ as there were ____________________ in the same year.

D. Look at the following graph which is a line graph. It shows the number of people who lived in Smithsville and in Capital City from 1960 to 1970.

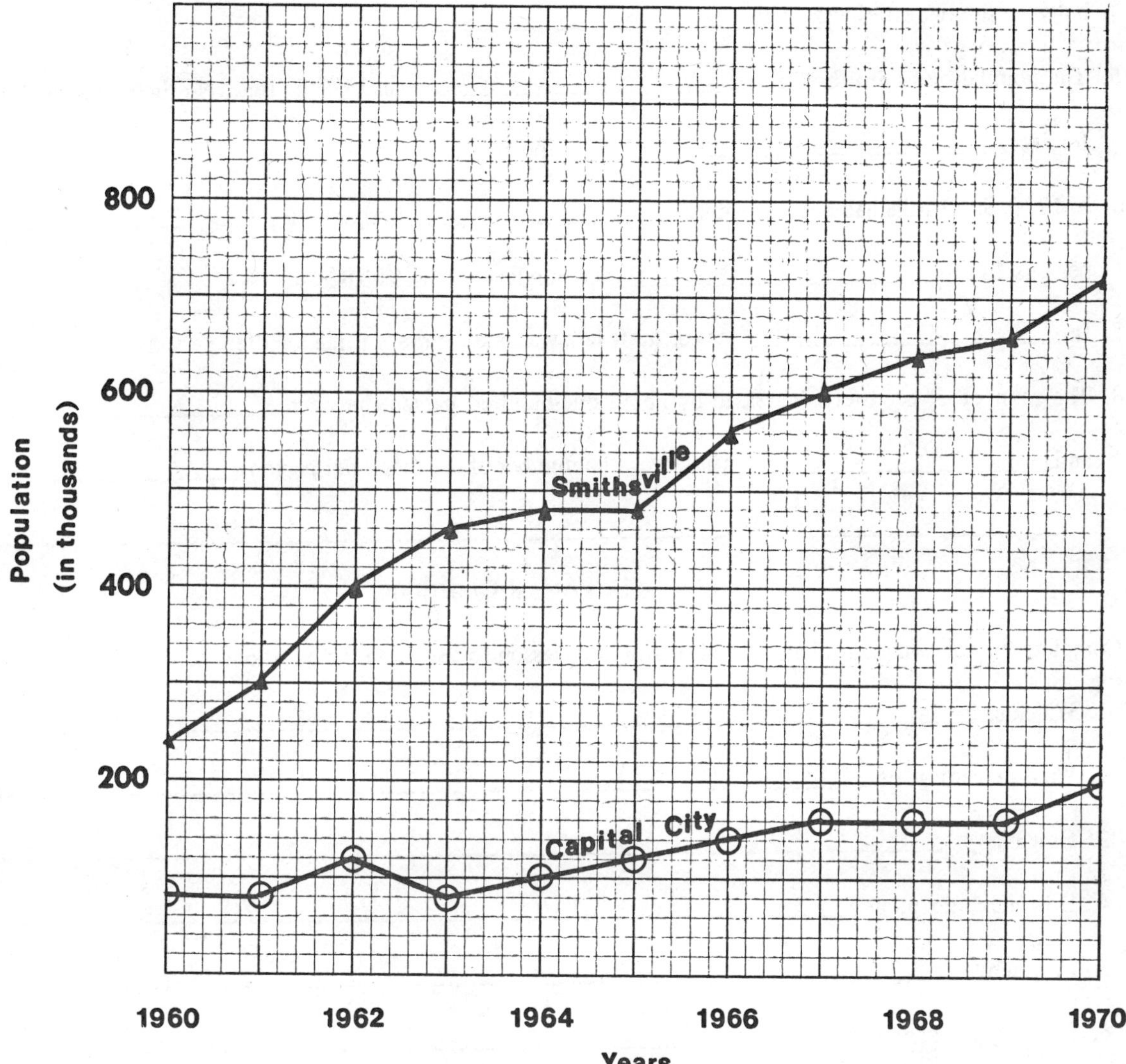

Complete the following sentences.

1. The population of Capital City rose from approximately ____________________ to approximately ____________________ in ____________________ years.

2. The population of Capital City increased fast between ____________________ and ____________________; however, the following year, it ____________________.

3. Between ____________________ and ____________________ the population of ____________________ doubled, but ____________________ it remained the same.

4. The population of ________________ was approximately fifty percent of that of ________________ in ________________; however, in ________________ the difference between the two cities was much ________________.

5. The population of Smithsville was ________________ in 1970; in that year there was one murder for every ________________ persons in the city.

6. In 1970, Smithsville had approximately ________________ burglaries for every ________________ persons, but in ________________ the burglary rate was higher.

7. In ________________ the car theft rate was one for every three-hundred persons.

8. The number of car thefts increased by about one-hundred percent between ________________ and ________________; however, the number of car thefts per person ________________ ________________.

Exercise 5: Logical Questions

A. Complete the following questions. Use ideas from this lesson to complete the questions.

1. Which city ________________?
2. What percentage of ________________?
3. How many ________________?
4. How much tax money ________________?
5. In which year ________________?
6. Which type of crime ________________?
7. How fast ________________?
8. How long ________________?
9. Between what two years ________________?
10. What was the average ________________ of ________________ in ________________ ________________?

B. Write four questions of *contrast* about the two cities.

1. What is the difference between the ______________________ in ______________________ and the ______________________ in ______________________?

2. How is ______________________ different from ______________________?

3. In what ways are ____ different?

4. How is ______________________ ______________________er than ______________________?

C. Write four questions of *comparison* about the two cities.

1. What are the similarities between the ______________________ in ______________________ and the ______________________ in ______________________?

2. How is ______________________ like ______________________?

3. How are the ______________________ who live in ______________________ similar to the ______________________ who live in ______________________?

4. How is/are the ______________________ in ______________________ the same as that/those in ______________________?

Questions of Contrast

What is the difference between *x* and *y*?

How / In what way(s) } is *x* different from *y*? / is *x* ______er than *y*?

Questions of Comparison

What are the similarities between *x* and *y*?

How / In what way(s) } is *x* like *y*? / is *x* similar to *y*? / is *x* the same as *y*?

Exercise 6: Oral Practice

A. Practice the following patterns aloud.

1. The city with the bustling streets was too noisy for the tourists.

   polluted

   busy

   dirty

   ugly

   crowded

2. The industrial city with the smoking chimneys wasn't clean enough for me.

   attractive

   quiet

   modern

3. Modern cities often have too many people.

   too many crowds.

   too many cars.

   too many germs.

   too many sick people.

   too many unhealthy people.

   too many angry people.

   too many nervous people.

   too many diseases.

4. The industrial city had too much noise.

   too much dirt.

   too much smoke.

   too much pollution in the air.

   too much pollution in the water.

5. The unpleasant city had too few pleasant places.

   too few quiet places.

   too few clean places.

   too few healthy people.

   too few happy people.

6. The industrial city had too little fresh air.

too little unpolluted air.

too little clean water.

too little unpolluted water.

too little sunshine.

too little quiet.

too little space.

B. 1. One city has happy citizens, and the other does too.

high taxes,

many churches,

a lake,

grocery stores,

2. One city doesn't have a king, and the other doesn't either.

a large airport,

a subway,

a water shortage,

an army,

3. One city has tall buildings, but the other doesn't

skyscrapers,

large factories,

air pollution,

a university,

4. One city doesn't have large crowds, but the other does.

polluted air,

crowded streets,

slums,

tall buildings,

C. 1. The noisy city made the citizens feel unhappy.

dirty	sick.
crowded	tired.
polluted	angry.
ugly	nervous.
	irritable.

2. The clean city made the people feel happy.

pleasant	relaxed.
attractive	friendly.
quiet	healthy.

3. The city which was dirty made the inhabitants sick.

which was ugly
which was crowded
which was polluted
which was noisy

4. The city which was pleasant made the citizens happy.

which was clean
which was quiet
which was attractive

D. Complete the following. Provide new vocabulary for each blank.

The	noisy	city	which had	too many people	made	the man	sick.
	______			too many ______		______	______.
	______			too many ______		______	______.
	______			too many ______		______	______.
	______			too much ______		______	______.
	______			too much ______		______	______.
	______			too few ______		______	______.
	______			too few ______		______	______.
	______			too little ______		______	______.
	______			too little ______		______	______.

E. Practice the following patterns.

1. The visitors wanted to visit the local museum.

    tried

    intended

    promised

    hoped

    expected

    agreed

    decided

2. The businessmen wanted the farmers to visit the downtown area.

    persuaded

    advised

    told

    expected

3. Complete the following.

    a. Politicians usually want ________________________ to vote for ________________________.

    b. Tourists want to ________________________ museums and to see ________________________.

    c. Cities should order ________________________ to ________________________ filters in factory chimneys.

    d. Advertisers try to ________________________ people to ________________________.

    e. Architects will usually agree to ________________________ in ________________________ cities.

Exercise 7: Favorable and Derogatory Opinions

Some opinions are favorable; some are derogatory (unfavorable). For example, "Modern architecture is ugly" is an unfavorable opinion. "Modern architecture is beautiful" is a favorable opinion.

Of course, not all statements are favorable or derogatory. Some statements are neither. Opinions can be *subjective* or *objective.* Subjective opinions tell how the speaker or writer feels about the topic.

Complete the following sentences. Each sentence uses a count/noncount expression.

too much	very much
too many	very many
too little	very little
too few	very few

Each sentence expresses an opinion.

1. Give the correct count/noncount words.
2. Indicate if the opinion is favorable or derogatory.

Example:

The city had too much noise. ______*derogatory*______

---

1. The industrial city had very ______________ polluted air. ______________
2. The small town has too ______________ happy people. ______________
3. The dirty city with too ______________ ______________
   germs had ______________ sick people.
4. The crowded city had very ______________ ______________
   sunshine and too ______________ pleasant parks.
5. The unhealthy city had too ______________ ______________
   polluted air, too ______________ noise
   and too ______________ crowds.

Exercise 8: Synonyms and Antonyms

Words with similar meanings are called *synonyms.* Words which have opposite meanings are called *antonyms.*

Rearrange these words into pairs of synonyms and pairs of antonyms.

thriving	industrial	rural
old	old-fashioned	citizen
residents	both	neither
downtown	ugly	in the suburbs
visitor	modern	inhabitants
narrow	attractive	new
bustling	quiet	wide
dirty	dying	polluted

Synonyms

__________	__________
__________	__________
__________	__________

Antonyms

__________	__________
__________	__________
__________	__________
__________	__________
__________	__________
__________	__________
__________	__________
__________	__________
__________	__________
__________	__________

Conversation Practice

Mr. Smith and Mr. Jones are both lawyers; the former practices in Capital City, and the latter in Smithsville. Mr. Smith wants his friend to move to Capital City in order to be his partner.

1. Complete the following phone conversation

   a. Try to use some of the following vocabulary.

very	want to ____	want ____ to ____	should
too	expect to ____	expect ____ to ____	can
enough	hope to ____	persuade ____ to ____	will
	refuse to ____	convince ____ to ____	might
	try to ____		may
			must

   b. Practice your conversation orally with a classmate.

Mr. Smith (answers phone): ____

____

____

Mr. Jones: ____

____

____

Mr. Smith (enthusiastic): ____

____

____

Mr. Jones: ____

____

____

Mr. Smith: I don't know why you want to stay in Smithsville. You should move to Capital City next year. It's cleaner, quieter, and more beautiful here. You're too nervous and irritable. You won't feel so nervous all the time here, and you won't fight with your wife so much.

Mr. Jones (annoyed): ______________________________

____

____

Mr. Smith (apologetic): ______________________________

____

____

Mr. Jones: ______________________________

____

____

Mr. Smith: ______________________________

____

____

Mr. Jones (enthusiastic): ______________________________

____

____

Mr. Smith (ends conversation): ______________________________

____

____

Writing

Exercise 1: Writing Sentences

A. Write sentences of comparison and contrast about Smithsville and Capital City.

1. ______________ is different from ______________ because ______________
____.

2. ______________ is like ______________ because ______________
____.

3. ______________, but ______________________________.

4. ______________, and ______________________________ too.

5. ______________, and ______________________________ either.

6. ______________ is ______________er than ______________.

7. ______________ is ______________ than ______________.

8. ______________ is as ______________ as ______________.

9. ______________ is not as ______________ as ______________.

10. ______________ is less ______________ than ______________.

11. ______________ has more ______________ than ______________.

12. ______________ is similar to ______________ because ______________
____.

13. Both ______________ and ______________ are ______________.

14. Neither ______________ nor ______________ is ______________.

15. ______________________; on the other hand, ______________
____.

16. ______________________; however, ______________
____.

17. ______________________; on the contrary, ______________
____.

B. Write two sentences about the two cities. Write sentences of *contrast* which are false.

1. ______________________________ *contrast false*

____

2. ______________________________ *contrast false*

____

C. Write two sentences of comparison about farmers and people who live in cities.

1. ______________________________ *comparison true*

____

2. ______________________________ *comparison true*

____

D. Write two sentences about any two places which you choose.

Your sentences may be comparison *or* contrast. They may be true or false.

1. ______________________________

____

2. ______________________________

____

Read your sentences aloud to the class. Ask the class to decide:

Is the sentence comparison or contrast?

Is the sentence true or false?

E. Answer the following questions.

1. What should people who live in a crowded city persuade the government to do?

____

____.

2. What should homeowners who live near a factory which pollutes the water refuse to do?

____

____

3. What can engineers do to help people who live in a city with many factories?

____

____.

4. What can architects do to make a city pleasant?

____

____.

5. What should the government plan to do in order to stop pollution from smoke?

____

____.

6. What should doctors advise the people who live in a dirty city to do?

____

____.

7. What should doctors convince the mayor of a noisy city to do?

____

____.

8. What can children do to make their city cleaner?

____

____.

9. What can students to do make a school cleaner?

____

____.

10. What can people do to make the parks in their cities more attractive?

____

____.

Exercise 2: Writing about Information—Comparison and Contrast

Study the pictures of life in an urban community and life in a rural community. Look for similarities and differences.

Unit 5
Writing

A. 1. Look at the buildings and their surroundings.

Use the following questions to make a list of differences and similarities.

Arc thc houses close together?

Do they have gardens?

Do they have trees for shade?

Do they have grass around them?

Do they have street lights?

Do they have traffic signs?

Are the houses tall, (one-storey, etc.)?

Are they close to the street?

Do they have fire escapes?

Are there any stores close by?

Do the people have a lot of open space?

Where do they park their cars?

Do the houses have places where people can sit out doors?

Is there an area for recreation? What kind?

Similarities
City and Country

____

____

____

____

____

Differences

City *Country*

____

____

____

____

____

____

2. Write a short paragraph about the differences between the buildings and general surroundings in the two places. Use vocabulary of contrast.

The city street differs from the country street in its buildings and general surroundings. ______________

____

____

____

____

____

____

____

____

____

____

____

____.

B. 1. Look at the activities on the two streets. Look at this list of the activities of the people who live on the two streets.

The lists are incomplete. Complete them.

Farm Lane	*Prospect St.*
swinging on a swing	carrying groceries
playing with a dog	playing ball
playing ball	riding a bike
washing a car	walking a pet dog
______________	shopping
______________	talking
	______________
	______________
	______________

2. Divide the lists into adults' activities and children's activities.

Farm Lane	*Prospect St.*
Activities of adults	Activities of adults
________________	________________
________________	________________
________________	________________
Activities of children	________________
________________	________________
________________	________________
________________	Activities of children
	________________
	________________
	________________

3. a. Are the children's activities in the two places similar or different? Separate them into two lists.

Similar activities	*Different activities*

b. What inferences can you make about children's activities in the two places? For example, what can't the children who live on Prospect St. do, but the rural children can? Make a list of inferences which are similarities and a list of inferences that are differences.

c. Look at the children's clothing. Do the children in the city street look like the country children?

d. Complete the following short paragraph. Use vocabulary of comparison.

On the whole, country children and city children look like each other and act like each other. They wear ______________________ clothing in both places. For example, ______________________

____ .

They play ______________________ games. The children who ______________________ like to

______________________________, and ______________________________ too.

Both rural and city children ____

____ .

4. a. Are the adult activities in the two places similar or different? Make two lists.

Similarities *Differences*

b. What inferences can you make about the activities of the grownups in the two places? For example, do the people in both places like plants? What can the city people do more easily than the people who live on Farm Lane? What different work must adults do in the two places? etc. Make two lists of your inferences, one for similarities and the other for differences.

c. Write a brief composition of comparison and contrast about activities in the two places. You may include both adults and children. Use examples and inferences. You should have two paragraphs: the first about similarities, and the second about differences. Use appropriate vocabulary of comparison and contrast.

Exercise 3: Semicolon and Comma

A. Study the following punctuation patterns for sentences of comparison and contrast.

– – – – – –, and – – – – – – –.

– – – – – –, but – – – – – – –.

– – – – – –; however, – – – – – –.

– – – – – –; on the other hand, – –.

– – – – – –; on the contrary, – – –.

– – – – – –. However, – – – – – –.

– – – – – –. On the other hand, – –.

– – – – – –. On the contrary, – – –.

1. What is the rule for *however*?
2. What is the rule for *on the other hand*?
3. What is the rule for *on the contrary*?
4. What cause and result vocabulary word has the same rule?

B. Punctuate the following sentences.

1. new highways do not necessarily bring benefits to the citizens of a community on the contrary they can do real harm by introducing more traffic into a district and increasing air pollution

___

___

___

___

2. shopping centers in the suburbs are convenient on the other hand they often replace open spaces which might be used for recreation

___

___

___

___

3. in the late nineteenth century the cities of the u s increased in number and size and farm production increased at a similar rate

____

____

____

____

4. modern cities with their tall skycrapers and bustling business districts seem to make good use of the available space however few people actually live in the downtown areas therefore valuable space is wasted everyday and elaborate transportation systems are necessary

____

____

____

____

5. the crime rate in many large cities is high but visitors who are careful shouldnt be afraid because most violent crimes take place between members of the same family you should visit my city but remember to leave your family at home

____

____

____

____

Exercise 4: Comparison and Contrast

Look at the illustrations. Make inferences about life in the two places.

Complete the following paragraphs of personal opinion.

A. Generally speaking, ______________ (urban/rural) communities are ______________ (less/more) convenient and ______________ (less/more) lonely for housewives than rural homes. Take ______________ (Prospect Street/ ______________ Farm Lane), for example. ______________________________

____

____

____

On the other hand, women who stay at home in houses like those on ______________________ can't

______________________. Unlike ______________________ housewives, they must ____________
city/rural

____________. They don't have ______________________. They need ______________________

____.

______________________ life may have some disadvantages, but for housewives the advantages are much greater.

B. City streets may be noisier and more crowded, but they are more friendly than less populated places, according to Pete, the owner of the grocery store on the corner of Prospect Street and Fifth Street. I ____________ agree/disagree/agree in part ____________. Consider Pete's own street, for example. It certainly is ______________________ than

______________________ because ____.

It's more crowded too. Last Saturday there were ______________________________________

____

____.

But is it a more friendly place? I ______________________ so. Let me explain, ______________
think/don't think

____

____

____.

C. Mr. Lawson is the owner of the house at 34 Farm Lane. Last week, he visited a cousin who lives on Prospect Street in the neighboring city. Mr. Lawson refused to take his children with him because, in his opinion, the city is too dangerous and unhealthy for children. He told his wife that city children lead different lives from children as fortunate as their own.

Look at the two illustrations. Do you agree or disagree with Mr. Lawson's opinion? Which is a better place for children to live? Write a short composition of comparison about children's lives in the two places.

1. Answer the following questions. Give examples. Make inferences.

   What do children wear?

   What kind of pets can they have?

   Is one place more healthy for children than the other?

   Is one place more dangerous for children than the other?

   Are children in one place more fortunate than those who live in the other?

2. Make a list of differences and similarities before you write.

3. Start with a generalization:

   The lives of city children and rural children are similar in some respects and different in others.

4. Give examples.

5. Use vocabulary of comparison and contrast.

6. End with a general statement of opinion about which children are more fortunate.

Exercise 5: Writing Description

A. Look at the illustration of the rural community.

Write sentences of comparison or contrast using the following expressions.

Example:

contrast

the dog which is running across the lawn — the pet cat

The dog which is running across the lawn is black and white, but the pet cat on the porch isn't.

---

1. *comparison*

the cat with the white fur — the dog without a collar

____

______________________________.

2. *comparison*

the woman on the porch steps — the girl near the trees

____

______________________________.

3. *comparison*

the man who is washing his car — his neighbor with the lawn mower

____

______________________________.

4. *contrast*

the barefoot boy — the boy with the striped shirt

____

______________________________.

5. *contrast*

the house with the picnic table — the two-storey house next door

____

______________________________.

B. Look at the illustration of the urban community. The following short paragraph is about Prospect Street. The sentences are too short and repetitious. Rewrite the paragraph combining some short sentences to make longer, more sophisticated sentences. Good paragraphs can have some short sentences and some long sentences too.

A woman is looking out her window. She has black hair. The window is in her apartment. She lives in the apartment. The apartment is above a grocery store. The grocery store is on the corner. The woman is watching some children. The children are not in school. Three boys are playing ball. One boy is throwing the ball. He has on a white shirt. He is wearing shorts. A girl is riding a bicycle. She is in the street. She is in front of the grocery store. She is wearing a dress. She is barefoot. It is a hot day. The other boys are watching. They are sitting on the sidewalk.

C. You are sitting beside a third storey window in a house directly opposite 86 Prospect St. You are looking out the window, watching the activities in the street. Describe the scene. Use vocabulary of spatial relationships.

in the middle of	parallel to	below
next to	to the left of	under
beside	across from	underneath
close to	between	along
in front of	on	toward
behind	above	away from
next door to	on the first floor, etc.	

It's a sunny day today, and Prospect Street is full of activity. I'm too sick to go out, but I can enjoy the scene from my bedroom window. Let me describe it to you. ____

D. You are the new owner of the house and property at 32 Farm Lane, just outside Capital City. Gardening is your favorite hobby. Before this year, you lived in an apartment in downtown Smithsville near the lake. You hated the apartment because it was too noisy and got so little sunlight that your plants died. Write a letter to your elderly aunt in another state to tell her about your new home. Describe the difference between your new home and your old apartment. Give details about 32 Farm Lane.

Use vocabulary of contrast. Use vocabulary of spatial relationships.

your address ↗ ______________________
↘ ______________________

date → ______________________

Dear Aunt Margaret,

Your loving niece,

Exercise 6: Interpreting Graphs and Tables

The following opinions are interpretations of the data in the graphs and tables. Do you agree/disagree with the interpretations? You may agree with only a part of the opinion. Explain your interpretation. Use (1) explicit examples from the statistics; (2) inferences which the statistics imply; (3) information and inferences about the reading selection and illustrations.

Use vocabulary of comparison and contrast, and vocabulary of cause and result.

A. Many people believe that Smithsville was more dangerous in 1970 than in the previous years because it had too many new businesses and industries. For example, the number of crimes increased from ______________ ___________ to ______________________ in _________________________________ years.

Also in the same period of time ____ .

In my opinion, this interpretation is _____________________________________. Let me explain.
accurate/inaccurate/only partly accurate

____

____

____

____

____

____

____

____

____

____

____

____

____

____

____

____

____

B. Statistics show a large increase in the population of Smithsville in the nineteen sixties; therefore, the people of the city had larger families. More and more children were born, and the city spent more and more money for schools. This theory about Smithsville's population and schools is ______________________.
accurate/inaccurate/only partly accurate
Let me explain my interpretation. ______________________

____

____

____

____

____

____

____

____

C. One year during the 1960s the number of crimes decreased in Smithsville, but the number of factories remained the same. Some of the older citizens who liked the city better in "the good old days" say, "It's the factory workers who come here from other places who cause all the trouble. They're the ones who steal the cars and murder people. The more outsiders we have, the more crime we have." In my opinion, this argument

______________________. Let me tell you why. ______________________
is nonsense/makes sense

____

____

____

____

____

____

____

____

____

____

____

Exercise 7: Letters of Opinion and Persuasion

This advertisement which appeared in newspapers throughout the country was paid for by the Smithsville Business Association.

> Industrial Enterprises
>
> Are you looking for a new home? Are you tired of paying high taxes?
>
> Bustling, energetic Smithsville, home of three worldwide chemical companies, with markets in 50 states and 17 foreign countries, welcomes new industry. Rail connections, air lines, good highways are waiting for your products. We have the land, and we have the labor force.
>
> Grow prosperous with us. Locate in Smithsville.

A. You are the secretary of a citizens' organization which opposes industrial growth in Smithsville. Your organization, Citizens for a Better Smithsville, does not want more people to come to Smithsville, wants to stop pollution, and wants the mayor to pass a law to prohibit any more building projects near the lake. Write a letter to the local newspaper, *The Smithsville Free Press,* protesting this advertisement and giving your reasons.

your address → ____________________

____

date → ____________________

The Editors
The Smithsville Free Press

Dear Sirs:

Sincerely yours,

your name → ____________________

your organization → ____________________

B. You are an influential legislator in Capital City. Last week you saw the Smithsville Business Association's ad in a newspaper, and later that week you learned that the ad persuaded your friend, a very wealthy clothing manufacturer, to visit the area in order to evaluate the location. You would like to persuade your friend to invest her money in Capital City instead. You want industries to come to Capital City, but you also want to preserve its small town atmosphere because you don't want to lose votes. You know that the citizens of Capital City might oppose any large-scale industrial development. Write a letter to your friend asking her to consider Capital City instead of Smithsville. You must choose your reasons carefully because you intend to send a copy of your letter to the president of the Capital City Preservation Club.

your ↗ ______________________
address ↘ ______________________

date → ______________________

______________________ ← your friend's name

______________________ ← her business address

Dear ______________________:

Sincerely yours,

your name → ______________________

cc. Chairperson, Capital City Preservation Club

Extra Vocabulary and Writing Practice

Exercise 1: Vocabulary Review

A. Give the correct form.

	Noun	*Verb*	*Adjective*
Example:	pollution	pollute	polluted
1.	______	produce	______
2.	______	______	prosperous
3.	force	______	______
4.	legislature	______	______
5.	______	inhabit	______
6.	______	grow	______
7.	dirt	______	______
8.	______	die	______
9.	______	attract	______
10.	______	connect	______

B. Use the correct form to complete the sentence. Practice the pronunciation of each sentence.

Example: pollution

Polluted air can cause disease.

Use the correct form of the appropriate word from this list.

prosperity	growing
relax	combination
transport	legislative
industry	

1. ____________________ claim that factories can make a community ____________________.
2. Two major sources of air pollution are ____________________ and industry.
3. Many people are worried about urban ____________________.
4. In order to solve urban problems there must be a ____________________ effort on the part of the ____________________ and the general public.
5. Cities should provide facilities for recreation and ____________________.

Exercise 2: Vocabulary and Spelling Review

Complete the following sentences.

1. Fac______ can be the cause of a lot of pollution; on the other h___, they can also be the s___ce of tax__ and em____ment.

2. R_________ of the suburbs are usually happy when the city builds sh___ing c_______.

3. Is the cr___ rate of large cit___ always hi__er than that of small towns?

4. Large cities often have t___ b____ings with mod___ a________ture downtown; however, vis_____ can usually find sl___ in the same n____bor____.

5. Heavy tr_____ and cr___ed streets are characteristic of most ___iving b___ling in_________ centers.

Exercise 3: Compositions

A. Write a composition about the differences between a real friend and an acquaintance.

1. Make a list of ideas first.

2. Organize the list into groups of ideas.

3. Start your composition with a generalization.

    Generally speaking, there are _______ main differences between a real friend and an acquaintance.

    or

    On the whole, a good friend is different from a person who is just an acquaintance.

    or

    Most people have a lot of acquaintances but very few real friends.

    or

    It is (isn't) difficult to tell the difference between a real friend and an acquaintance.

4. Give examples. Give details from your own experience.

5. Use vocabulary of comparison and contrast.

    Which kind of vocabulary will you use more—comparison or contrast?

6. Use words like:

need	expect____to	can	very____
lend	persuade____to	will	too____
borrow	help____to	may	____enough
help	care about____	must	so____that____
give	take care of____	might	make____happy
		should	
		ought to	

B. In your opinion, which is more convenient–a house in the suburbs or an apartment in the middle of a city? Write a composition of comparison and contrast.

1. Start with a generalization.

   Living in a house in the suburbs is more convenient than living in a city apartment.

   or

   A city apartment is more convenient than a house in the suburbs.

2. Give examples. (Make lists of advantages and disadvantages first.) Give specific details about both kinds of homes.

3. Use vocabulary of comparison and contrast. Use vocabulary of cause and result. Which vocabulary will you use more–comparison or contrast? How much of your composition should be about similarities?

4. Try to use vocabulary from this unit and earlier units.

C. Where do you prefer to go for your vacation–to a city or to the country? Why?

Write a composition of contrast about a vacation in the city and a vacation in the country.

1. Make a list of differences.

2. Organize your list into groups.

3. Start with a generalization which gives your opinion.

4. Use vocabulary of contrast.

D. Write a composition about two cities, your own hometown and another city.

1. Make a list of similarities.

2. Make a list of differences.

3. Organize your two lists into main points and examples. Be sure you have examples for your main ideas.

4. Write a composition of comparison and contrast about the two cities. Use appropriate vocabulary. Begin your composition with a generalization. Give examples and specific descriptions of the two cities.

> ____________ and ____________ have many characteristics in common; however, the differences between these two cities are more important.
>
> **or**
>
> ____________ and ____________ are different in some minor respects, but their similarities are far more important to me.

E. Choose two persons whom you know or know about; they can be members of your family, or famous people, or your friends.

Write a composition in which you compare and contrast the two persons.

1. Choose the two people carefully. They should have some similarities and some differences. How do they act? What do they do? What do they look like? etc.

2. Organize your ideas.

3. Start your composition with a generalization.

4. Give examples. Give details. You may want to use examples in chronological order, and you may want to include a description of each person's appearance.

5. Use vocabulary of comparison and contrast.

6. Review earlier units for appropriate vocabulary.

Unit 6: Reading

Lucky George

"Today is going to be a lucky day for me," announced George Beckstone as he drank his first cup of coffee. "The first cup of coffee in the morning is always the best," he thought. "Everything is going to be fine."

His wife, Muriel, a fat woman with black curly hair and a round moonlike face, was frying eggs at the stove. "You're a fool," she said loudly, looking at the stove but talking to George just the same. "Just a superstitious old fool. The only reason you feel lucky is because it's Friday and you don't go to the office on Saturdays." She turned around and glared at George.

"You're happy because you think you are going to play golf all day with Willie," she shouted. "Well, let's get one thing straight. Tomorrow you're going to clean the basement first." She banged the eggs on the table and lit a cigarette. She blew smoke in George's face.

George looked at the eggs and then at his wife. He didn't like eggs very much especially the way Muriel cooked them, and he didn't like cigarette smoke especially in the morning. But Muriel was different. A man likes some things and loves others. A man doesn't like some things, but other things he just hates. George hated Muriel. According to George, life with Muriel was not worth living. Today was going to be lucky–lucky for George. George was going to kill Muriel.

Exercise 1: Reading for Explicit and Implicit Information

This story tells us some information directly. It tells us the day, the time of day, the people's names, and so on. When a passage gives us information directly, we say the information is *explicit.* When a passage doesn't give us information directly, but we can make inferences, we say the information is *implicit.*

A. Read the following questions. Are the answers explicit or implicit in the story?

1. What is the man's name? ______*explicit*______
2. Is he married? ____________
3. What day was it? ____________
4. What does he like to drink in the morning? ____________
5. Was that day a typical day in George's life? ____________
6. Why does George hate Muriel? ____________
7. Why is Muriel critical of George? ____________
8. Who is the boss in the family? ____________
9. Is Muriel a pleasant woman? ____________
10. Why did Muriel talk about the dirty basement? ____________

11. Is George a fool? ____________________

12. Was George really planning a murder? ____________________

B. Muriel dislikes George. How do we know? What does she do? What does she say? Find some words and phrases in the story that tell us *explicitly* that Muriel doesn't like George.

____________________ ____________________

____________________ ____________________

C. What is Muriel's opinion of George? How do you know? Is the information explicit or implicit in the story?

Read the following sentences. Indicate *true* or *false, explicit* or *implicit* for each.

Example:

According to Muriel, George is foolish. ______*true*______

______*explicit*______

---

1. Muriel thinks George is selfish and inconsiderate. ____________________

____

2. Muriel considers George likeable. ____________________

____

3. Muriel considers George lucky. ____________________

____

4. She thinks her husband is irresponsible. ____________________

____

5. According to Muriel, George is hardworking. ____________________

____

6. In Muriel's opinion, George is old. ____________________

____

7. According to Muriel, the basement is dirty. ____________________

____

8. In George's opinion, coffee is enjoyable in the morning, but cigarette smoke isn't. ____________________

____

Exercise 2: Making Inferences

A. Read the following information. The information is not well organized; it's not in chronological sequence.

1. The police doctor said, "This woman died about 8 a.m. today, approximately four hours ago."
2. On Saturday at 10:30 a.m., the Beckstones' neighbor, Mrs. Herbert, knocked on the backdoor of the Beckstones' house. Nobody answered the door.
3. Muriel's mother discovered her daughter at the bottom of the basement steps. Muriel was dead.
4. On Saturday at 11:45 a.m. Muriel's mother arrived at the Beckstones' house. She knocked on the back door. Nobody answered, but the door wasn't locked. She went in the house.
5. The police talked to Muriel's mother.
6. At noon the police arrived at the Beckstone house.
7. Mrs. Herbert informed a policeman that George left in his car about 8 a.m. She always heard the Beckstones' car because their driveway was next to her kitchen.
8. George's mother-in-law told a policeman that George always played golf on Saturday morning. She assumed that he was at the golf club.
9. At noon George was playing golf with his friend, Willie.
10. The police detective called the golf course and talked to George.
11. Mrs. Herbert remembered the Beckstones' kitchen light was on at 8:30 a.m. She noticed it from her bedroom window.
12. George told the detective he left his house about 7:30 a.m. He went to pick up Willie at Willie's house. Then they went to the golf course.
13. Muriel's mother said the kitchen light was off at 11:45 a.m., but the basement light was on.
14. Mrs. Herbert was very curious. She ran over to the house next door and asked the policeman, "Can I help?"

B. *Inferences*

From this information about Saturday morning we can make some inferences.

Complete the following inferences. Choose the appropriate vocabulary from the list.

murder	according to	die
murderer	alibi	dead
witness	accident	death
policeman	accidental	solve
police	observe	solution
details	observant	give evidence
clues	crime	take (down) evidence
innocent	guilty	

1. Mrs. Herbert is probably a good ________________ because she is very curious and ________________.

2. The ________________ probably ________________ ________________ the evidence in his notebook.

3. The police detective thinks that George ________________ Muriel, so he is looking for ________________.

4. ________________ ________________ George, he and Willie were playing golf all morning, but the ________________ are probably going to check his ________________.

5. The police need more ________________ in order to ________________ the crime and arrest the ________________ person.

6. Muriel's mother probably thinks George is ________________.

7. The police are probably going to find out that Muriel's ________________ was ________________ .

Exercise 3: Logical Questions

A. In order to solve the problem of Muriel's death, the police asked a lot of questions.

Here are some answers.

Who answered the question?

What was the question? Who do you think asked it?

Example:

Answer: "This woman died about 8 a.m. today."

Speaker: The police doctor gave this answer.

Question/Questioner: A policeman asked, "When did this woman die?"

---

1. Answer: "I found her. The door wasn't locked, so I came in."

   Speaker: ______________________________

   Question/Questioner: ______________________________

2. Answer: "He's at the golf course."

   Speaker: ______________________________

   Question/Questioner: ______________________________

3. Answer: "He picked me up around eight."

   Speaker: ______________________________

   Question/Questioner: ______________________________

4. Answer: "At 8:30 a.m."

   Speaker: ______________________________

   Question/Questioner: ______________________________

5. Answer: "I'm George Beckstone."

   Speaker: ______________________________

   Question/Questioner: ______________________________

B. In order to solve the problem of Muriel's death, the police need additional information. They know the kind of questions they need to ask and the kind of answers they want to get.

Here is a list of the kind of answers they need. Write the appropriate questions.

	Question	*Kind of Answer*
1.	______________________________?	reason
2.	______________________________?	from *time* to *time*
3.	______________________________?	person
4.	______________________________?	place
5.	______________________________?	a measurement

C. There are many things the police don't know about Muriel's death. You are a police detective. Write five questions you want to ask George.

1. ______________________________?
2. ______________________________?
3. ______________________________?
4. ______________________________?
5. ______________________________?

Exercise 4: Relevant and Irrelevant Information

A. The police asked a lot of questions. Some were obvious, but others weren't. Some seemed stupid, but others didn't. Read the following questions. Indicate if the question is relevant or irrelevant.

1. What did Muriel eat for breakfast? ____________
2. Why was Mrs. Herbert watching the Beckstones' kitchen? ____________
3. How far is Willie's house from the golf course? ____________
4. Who won the game of golf? ____________
5. Did George stay at the golf course all morning? ____________
6. What kind of shoes was Muriel wearing? ____________
7. Did Muriel have a lot of money? ____________
8. How old was Muriel? ____________
9. Was the basement clean? ____________
10. What did Muriel's mother do from 11:45 a.m. to noon? ____________

B. Indicate why you decided that certain questions are relevant or irrelevant to the investigation. Choose five.

Example:

I think the sixth question is relevant because maybe Muriel fell because of her shoes.

or

I think the sixth question is relevant because Muriel might have fallen because of her shoes.

---

1. ____
2. ____
3. ____
4. ____
5. ____

Exercise 5: Oral Practice

A. Use the appropriate verb form. Check the time for each item. Make sure your sentence is reasonable according to the information you have.

1. Time: It's Friday afternoon.

   George ate eggs for breakfast on Friday.

   ________________ on Saturday.

   ________________ every day.

   ________________ now.

2. Time: It's Friday a.m.

   Muriel smokes a cigarette every morning.

   ______________ now.

   ______________ on Saturday morning.

   ______________ yesterday.

3. Time: It's Friday a.m.

   George isn't going to play golf this afternoon.

   ________________ tomorrow morning.

   ________________ on Saturdays.

   ________________ yesterday.

4. Time: It's Friday.

   George is feeling lucky now.

   ____________ yesterday.

   ____________ next Saturday.

   ____________ every day.

B. There are many things the police don't know about Muriel's death. Use the following pattern to complete the sentences.

Example:

Who killed Muriel? The police don't know who killed Muriel.

Why did Muriel die? The police don't know why Muriel died.

---

1. Who turned out the kitchen light?	The police don't know who ______________ .
2. When did George ______?	The police don't know when ______________ .
3. ______ was George at the golf course?	__________ how long ______________ .
4. Why did Muriel ______ to the basement?	__________ why ______________ .
5. Who unlocked the ______?	__________ who ______________ .
6. How far is it to the golf course ______ Muriel's house?	__________ how far ______________ .
7. Which person will inherit Muriel's ______?	__________ which person ______________ .
8. Why is Mrs. Herbert ______?	__________ why ______________ .

C. There are many things the police don't know about Muriel's death.

Example:

Did George hate Muriel? The police don't know whether George hated Muriel or not.
The police don't know if he hated Muriel or not.

Use the pattern with *whether* or *if* for yes/no questions.

1. Did George return ______ between 7:30 and 8:30?	The police don't know if __________.
2. Did Mrs. Herbert ______ the truth?	whether ______.
3. Did Muriel ______ accidentally?	if __________.
4. Did George push his wife ______ the stairs?	if __________.
5. Did Muriel intend to ______ the basement herself?	whether ______.
6. Did Muriel have a big ______ insurance policy?	whether ______.

D. Use *while* and *during* to complete the following sentences.

Example:

Muriel smoked while George was eating.

Muriel smoked during breakfast.

---

1. Muriel's mother arrived at the house while George ______________________ golf.

   ______________________ during George's game.

2. George annoyed Muriel while they were married.

   ______________________ during ______________________.

3. The policeman examined the room while Muriel's mother was telephoning.

   ______________________ during ______________________.

4. George planned his alibi while he was driving.

   ______________________ during ______________________.

5. Mrs. Herbert was curious while the police were investigating the death.

   ______________________ during ______________________.

Exercise 6: Chronological Order

A. Chronological order is very important to the police. Read the following sentences. Each sentence is about chronological order.

Check your information. Is the statement true? Is the statement false? Will the police need additional information?

Example:

The kitchen door was locked at 11:45 a.m. ______ *false* ______

---

1. Mrs. Herbert saw a light in Muriel's kitchen after 8 a.m. ______________
2. George drove to Willie's house about 8:30 a.m. ______________
3. Muriel died sometime between 7 a.m. and 9 a.m. ______________
4. The light in Muriel's kitchen was on after 9 a.m. ______________
5. Somebody turned the kitchen light off between 8:30 and 11:45 a.m. ______________

6. The basement light was on at 8 a.m. ________________

7. George was at the golf course all morning from 8 a.m. to noon. ________________

8. Mrs. Herbert knocked at the Beckstones' door before 11 a.m. ________________

9. George killed Muriel and then drove to his friend's house at 7:30 a.m. ________________

10. Muriel turned off the kitchen light after 8:30 a.m., and later she fell down the basement stairs. ________________

B. Complete the following sentences. Choose the correct time word according to the evidence.

Example:

George ate his breakfast ___*before*___ he went to work on Friday.
before/after/when

---

1. Muriel wanted her husband to clean the basement ________________ he played golf.
before/after/when
2. Muriel's mother arrived ________________ George was playing golf with his friend.
while/during
3. Somebody turned off the kitchen light ________________ George's mother-in-law arrived.
before/after
4. George was at the golf course ________________ the policeman called.
until/after
5. Somebody turned the basement light on ________________ the morning.
when/during
6. Muriel's mother stayed in the house alone with her dead daughter ________________ the police came.
until/when
7. Mrs. Herbert was in her kitchen ________________ George was backing his car out of his driveway.
while/during
8. George picked up Willie ________________ he went to the golf course.
before/after
9. The police doctor examined the dead woman ________________ the other policeman talked to Muriel's mother on the phone.
after/while/before
10. Mrs. Herbert observed a light in her neighbor's kitchen ________________ she went to visit Muriel.
prior to/before/after/until
11. Mrs. Herbert was so curious ________________ the police arrived that she offered to help them.
when/while/during
12. George played golf for several hours ________________ 8 a.m. and noon
during/between
________________ the morning ________________ his wife was lying dead at the
while/during after/before/while
bottom of the basement stairs.

More Chronological Order Vocabulary	
before ____	prior to ____
after ____	during ____
until ____	until ____
while ____	for ____
when ____	between ____ and ____

Conversation Practice

Complete the following dialog between a policeman and Muriel's mother. Practice the dialog with a classmate. "Perform" your dialog for the class.

Mother: I'm so glad you are here. Please hurry. I think she's dead.

Policeman: O.K., O.K. Just keep calm. Where is she?

Mother (crying): ____________________

Policeman: When did you arrive at the house? How did you get in?

Mother: ____________________

Policeman: Did you notice anything unusual?

Mother: Unusual? There she was lying at the bottom of the stairs. Of course, it was unusual. Why don't you do something?

Policeman: ____________________

____

Mother: ____________________

____

Policeman: Where's her husband? Do you know? ____________________

Mother: ____________________

____

Policeman: ____________________

____

Mother: ____________________

____

Writing

Exercise 1: Writing Sentences

A. 1. Write three sentences of chronological order which are *true* according to the evidence.

a. ______________________ after ______________________.

b. ______________________ while ______________________.

c. ______________________ before ______________________.

2. Write three sentences of chronological order which are *false* according to the evidence.

a. ______________________ after ______________________.

b. ______________________ until ______________________.

c. ______________________ when ______________________.

B. Complete the following sentences of cause and result.

1. George said, "I couldn't have killed my wife because ______________________

______________________."

2. Muriel's mother supposed that Muriel might have ______________________

______________________ because ______________________.

3. The police suspected that George killed Muriel because ______________________

______________________.

4. Muriel's mother couldn't have killed her daughter because ______________________

______________________.

5. Mrs. Herbert ______________________;

therefore, George might have ______________________.

6. In my opinion, ______________________ must have ______________________

______________________ because ______________________.

7. ______________________; therefore, the

police ______________________.

8. ______________________ after ______________________;

therefore, ______________________ didn't tell the truth.

9. ______________________ before ______________________ ,

so ______________________ must have ______________________ .

10. ______________________ didn't realize that ______________________ ,

so ______________________ .

Exercise 2: Writing about Information—Chronological Order

The information about the events of Saturday morning is very confusing. Summarize the information according to chronological order. Use the past tense. Do not copy the sentences; change some of them; join some together with vocabulary of chronological order.

Use some of the following:

before – – –	before ____	first, – – etc.	at ____
after – – –	after ____	subsequently, – – –	from ____ to ____
when – – –	during ____	later, – – –	for ____
while – – –	prior to ____		between ____ and ____
until – – –	until ____		

How many paragraphs should your composition have?

Exercise 3: Chronological Order—Cause and Result

A. At first the police concluded that Muriel's death was an accident. Write a paragraph explaining why you agree or disagree with their conclusion.

The police think Muriel's death was accidental, but/and I ________________ with their conclusion. Let me explain my reasons.

____

____

____

____

____

____

____

____

____

____

____

____

____

B. The police discovered one additional piece of information.

1. Choose *one* piece of evidence from the following list.

   Mrs. Herbert is a little deaf.

   or

   George's watch is fast.

   or

   The light bulb in the kitchen burned out sometime during the morning.

   or

   Willie left George for about forty-five minutes during their game.

2. Use one additional piece of information to decide whether Muriel's death was accidental or not.

3. Use vocabulary of chronological order and vocabulary of cause and result to complete the following composition.

The police discovered that ____.

On the basis of this additional information, I expect them to prove that ______________________

____. Let me explain why.

____

____

____

____

____

____

____

____

____

Exercise 4: Punctuating Clauses

A. Examine the punctuation of the following sentences. Notice which sentences have commas.

1. a. When the police found new evidence, George confessed that he murdered his wife.

   b. George confessed that he murdered his wife when the police found new evidence.

2. a. Because one neighbor was observant, the police solved the crime.

   b. The police solved the crime because one neighbor was observant.

3. a. While the witness was talking, the policeman searched for clues.

   b. The policeman searched for clues while the witness was talking.

4. a. After the police warned George that he must notify them of his whereabouts, he assured them that he wouldn't leave town.

   b. George assured the police that he wouldn't leave town after they warned him that he must notify them of his whereabouts.

B. Punctuate the following sentences.

1. the suspect repeated the same story over and over when the police questioned him

2. the criminal didnt regret his actions until the police announced his arrest

3. because many people are unobservant we shouldnt assume that what witnesses tell us is necessarily true

4. after he learned that Muriel was dead her lawyer called George to remind him that she had a large life insurance policy however George was not pleased because the lawyer also informed the police

5. because Muriels mother doubted that George was telling lies she urged the police to stop the investigation but they refused

Exercise 5: Paraphrase

When we repeat *exactly* what someone says, we are quoting directly. In written form we must use quotation marks. For example, when the police detective quotes exactly what George says, he will use quotation marks in his report. In the same way, when we quote directly from a book or periodical, we must put quotation marks around the words, phrases, or sentences we copy.

However, it isn't always possible to carry around a tape recorder or a note book. Often we don't need to quote *exactly* what we hear or read. We can repeat what we heard or read in our own words. *Paraphrasing* is repeating in the listener's or reader's own words what he heard or read. Of course, a good paraphrase should be accurate.

Phrases for Introducing a Paraphrase or Summary

In other words, ______. To paraphrase, ------	Use *after* the passage you are paraphrasing.
In brief, --------- Briefly, ---------	Use when your paraphrase is short.
In summary, ------- To summarize, ------	Use when your paraphrase covers the entire passage, and gives all the main points.
On the whole, ------ Generally speaking, ----	Use when your paraphrase gives a generalization, or the main point(s).

For paraphrase we can use indirect speech and verbs like:

explain	announce	promise
mention	reply	know
point out	respond	believe
admit	tell	doubt
suggest	assure	imagine
write	notify	think
report	inform	

We can also use the phrase:

according to ______________________.

A. The day after Muriel's death, the following article appeared in the local paper.

Yesterday morning, death came suddenly to an attractive suburban housewife. Muriel Beckstone, a former school teacher at Wadely Elementary School, was found dead at the bottom of a steep flight of stairs by her mother. Police arrived quickly on the scene and notified George Beckstone, the deceased's husband. Mr. Beckstone, an employee of Strand Insurance Company, said his wife intended to clean the basement. Funeral arrangements will be announced tomorrow.

Write a brief paraphrase of the article. Give only the most important information.

____

____

____

B. In exercise 3 you wrote a solution to Muriel's death. Your solution was fairly long.

1. Write a summary statement of your solution. This summary would come at the end of your composition.

   To summarize, ________________________________

   ____

   ____

2. a. Read your solution of Muriel's death from exercise 3 aloud to the class.

   b. Ask your classmates to paraphrase your solution briefly. Check the paraphrases.

C. 1. Read the following about home accidents.

Many people worry about dying in a car accident or on a plane trip. They take all kinds of precautions when they travel, including taking out travel insurance at the airport. Yet most people are safer on the highway or on board a jet than they are in their own homes. Did you realize that more accidents occur at home than anywhere else? Housewives fall off ladders, fall down steep stairs, and burn themselves cooking. Children are burned, scalded, break bones, die in old refrigerators, and stick their fingers in light sockets. Fathers cut themselves on tools, set fire to themselves and their homes with cigarettes. Some people even drown in the bath tub. Your home may be the most dangerous place you'll ever be.

2. Summarize the main points of the article. Paraphrase. Don't copy.

____

____

____

____

Extra Vocabulary and Writing Practice

Exercise 1: Vocabulary Review

A. 1. Give the correct form for the following pairs of nouns and verbs.

2. Practice the pronunciation of each pair.

Noun	*Verb*
agreement	agree
promise	________________
________________	announce
________________	repeat
death	________________
imagination	________________
conclusion	________________
________________	discover
________________	hope
belief	________________
________________	decide
answer	________________
________________	report
announcement	________________
information	________________
solution	________________
knowledge	________________
________________	think
suggestion	________________

Exercise 2: Vocabulary and Spelling Review

1. Many people d__ in car ____dents on U.S. highways every year; such _________al d_____ are often totally unnecessary ______ing to traffic engineers.

2. The police always consider the ___dence very carefully before they arrest a suspect for ___der.

3. Super_________ people think some numbers are l___y and others are un_____.

4. In my op_____, George's wife ___liked him because she thought he was self___.

5. I think smokers are in___sider___ because they bl__ smoke in people's f____.

Exercise 3: Compositions

A. Write a composition about an exciting experience you once had. Describe the events in chronological order and explain why they happened. Use vocabulary of chronological order and vocabulary of cause and result.

B. Some people are very superstitious. They believe in lucky numbers, lucky days, etc. Write a short composition about superstitious people.

   1. Start with a generalization.

   2. Give examples.

   3. Explain your opinion about superstitions. Give reasons. Use vocabulary of cause and result. (Note: your examples should be relevant to your opinions.)

C. Read your composition on superstitions to the entire class. The class must listen very carefully while you are reading but should not take any notes. After you finish, ask the members of the class to write a brief paraphrase of your opinions on superstitions. Check their paraphrases. Are they fairly accurate?

D. Choose a famous historical person. Tell in your own words what he/she did and why people consider him/her important.

   1. Make a list of ideas first.

   2. Organize your ideas according to chronological order, and cause and result. You may also want to use classification and/or comparison and contrast.

   3. Ask your teacher to check your plan before you write.

   4. Start with a generalization about the person.

   5. Try to use a variety of vocabulary of relationships. For example, use different expressions for cause and result; don't use *because* each time.

Unit 7: Reading

Going Home Again

Last summer I had to go on a business trip which took me near the town I had lived in when I was a young boy growing up. I have a lot of happy memories of the good times I used to have there, so I thought I'd like to visit the old, familiar places again. I called up a boyhood pal, Joe Evans, who still lives there. Joe's in business too, is married, and has a great crowd of children. I knew this, although I hadn't seen him for years, because every year I get a card from him at Christmas. It's always the same kind of card, with a photograph of smiling Evans children in pajamas under a droopy Christmas tree. Sometimes there's a dog too. I used to be fond of Joe, but I had no intention of spending my one evening back home in the bosom of his family, with yelling kids and barking dogs. Besides, I'm allergic to dog hair.

Joe was eager to see me, too, but was very hesitant when I insisted that we spend the evening retracing the steps of my boyhood days. Maybe I sounded too sentimental, or maybe his wife doesn't let him go out at night, I thought, after I hung up.

We met at the train station. I recognized Joe at once despite his bald head and fat stomach. "Are you sure you wouldn't rather come home and meet Ellie and the kids?" he asked. "I've got a lot of old photographs of your family and mine when we used to live on Church Street. I think you'll. . . ."

"No, no. Thanks anyway, but let's go," I interrupted. "Right around the corner ought to be the Railway Hotel. Remember the senior dance there? Let's start off there with a drink." I hurried on around the corner, but where the handsome old hotel used to stand, there stretched a large ugly parking lot. Joe merely shrugged his shoulders, but I was furious. Why would anybody want to tear down the best example of turn-of-the-century architecture in the county? I glowered at the parking lot attendant, who looked puzzled, poor man, and strode off toward the main street with Joe puffing along half a step behind me. I was heading for the Home Bakery Coffee Shop, where I used to eat the best chocolate cake I've ever tasted. All the high school students used to go there every Saturday night. It was like a community ritual. That's where I had my very first date with a pretty little blonde girl; I can't remember her name. Joe caught up with me just as I reached the boarded-up store front. "Been out of business for five years, Tom," he said. "They couldn't compete with the chain stores."

That's how it went. The old school had been replaced by a modern building that looks exactly like a warehouse. The church we used to go to had burned down. Church Street had disappeared to make room for a four-lane highway.

Guess where I spent most of the evening. That's right. At Joe's, looking at a lot of faded pictures, and picking dog hairs off my new suit jacket. I never did get a piece of chocolate cake, and I sneezed for a month afterward.

Exercise 1: Reading for Information

A. Answer the following questions.

1. Does Tom approve or disapprove of Joe and Joe's family? Circle the words or phrases that tell you Tom's opinion of Joe.

2. Does Tom have a good sense of humor or is he a solemn person? How do you know?

3. Does Tom think he is superior to Joe? How do you know?

4. Do Tom and his friend have similar interests? What kinds of things do they each care about?

5. Which of the two men would you prefer to spend a day with? Why?

B. Look at your answers to the above questions.

1. For which questions was the information explicit in the reading selection?

2. For which questions was the information implied?

3. Look at your answer for the fifth question. How did you decide on your answer? Did you use explicit information, implicit information, information which is not in the reading selection?

Exercise 2: Reading for Logical Organization

A. The reading selection in this unit is a story which is told in the first person. Let's look at how the story is organized.

1. Most narratives are told in chronological order. Is the general organization of the story in chronological order? How do you know?

2. Organize the narrative into a chronological sequence. Make a list of the most important events of Tom's visit using:

   First,

   Next,

   Then,

   Afterward,

   After _______,

   Finally,

3. The general organization of this story is apparently chronological order, but the story also includes some comparison and a great deal of contrast. Make a list of some of the contrasts in the selection.

4. This reading selection also includes some explanations of cause and result. Make a list of some of the cause and result information in the selection.

Cause	*Result*

B. Some sentence patterns in English combine both chronological order and contrast. Look at the following sentences.

Decide which are: chronological order only

contrast only

both chronological order and contrast

neither contrast nor chronological order

Examples:

Tom used to dance at the old hotel, but he doesn't anymore. — *both chronological order and contrast*

The hotel was near the train station. — *neither contrast nor chronological order*

---

1. Tom studied architecture in college before he went into business. ____________

2. The coffee shop used to compete profitably with other businesses, but it can't now. ____________

3. Tom doesn't care for dogs because he is allergic to their hair. ____________

4. Tom had pleasant memories of his hometown; however, his return visit made him feel disappointed. ____________

5. Church Street was a residential street at one time, but today it is a highway filled with traffic instead of family homes. ____________

6. A splendid example of the architecture of former days used to stand around the corner from the train station, but it has been replaced by an ugly parking lot. ____________

C. Some sentence patterns in English combine both time (chronological order) and comparison. Look at the following sentences.

Decide which are: chronological order only

comparison only

both chronological order and comparison

neither chronological order nor comparison

Example:

Joe used to be interested in photography as an adolescent, and he still is today as a mature married man. *both chronological order and comparison*

---

1. Tom used to like chocolate cake, and he still does. ______

2. The new school looks like a warehouse, according to Tom, who is fonder of old-fashioned architecture than of modern architecture. ______

3. The town was no longer like it used to be; it was less attractive, more crowded, and less friendly than in the past. ______

4. Tom still likes Joe somewhat; on the other hand, he doesn't like Joe's pets or Joe's hobbies, but he never did. ______

5. Joe was hesitant because he knew that Tom might be disappointed. ______

6. Returning home after a long absence is often a disappointing experience. ______

Vocabulary which combines chronological order and contrast

– – – – used to – – –
– – – – no longer – – –
anymore (with negative)

Vocabulary which combines chronological order and comparison

– – – – used to – – – –
still

Note: Other time expressions and vocabulary of comparison or contrast can be combined in sentences or in pairs of sentences.

Exercise 3: Point of View

A. People can have different opinions about the same event. Although Tom and Joe spent the evening together, they didn't have the same reactions to what happened. Their points of view were different.

Complete the following sentences.

1. Tom felt ______________________________, but Joe, on the other hand, ______________________________.
2. Tom thought Joe looked ______________________________, but Joe might not agree.
3. Tom was annoyed because ______________________________, however, his friend ______________________________.
4. Joe thought that Tom ______________________________; on the contrary, Tom ______________________________.
5. Joe's reaction to ______________________________ was different from Tom's, because although they had ______________________________ the same ______________________________, they ______________________________.
6. Although Joe ______________________________, Tom ______________________________.
7. According to Tom, the old hotel ______________________________, but the town government ______________________________.
8. According to the parking lot attendant, ______________________________, but Tom ______________________________.
9. According to Joe, the chain stores ______________________________, but many businessmen thought the old bakery ______________________________.
10. From Joe's point of view, his annual Christmas photograph ______________________________, but Tom ______________________________.

B. 1. Tom used to like his old hometown. In fact, he was eager to revisit it. Do you think his opinion has changed since his visit? Make an inference about his opinion now.

Tom used to ______________________________, but

nowadays he has a different opinion. Now, according to Tom, his hometown is ______________

______________________________.

2. Tom and Joe had been friends for many years. Do you think their opinion of each other has changed since Tom's visit? What do you infer is Joe's opinion of his friend Tom now?

Nowadays Joe thinks that Tom ______________________________.

3. What descriptive words might Joe use to describe Tom to a stranger?

____

____

____

Would Tom agree? Do you think Tom's opinion of himself would be the same as Joe's? Would Joe use the same terms to describe Tom to his wife as he would to a stranger? Why not?

When we speak confidentially, we don't say the same things or use the same words as when we are speaking to people we don't know very well.

C. The story is told from Tom's point of view.

Discuss the following questions.

1. Who would tell the story differently? What changes would Ellie make? What changes in the story would Joe make?

2. Is Tom telling the story to Joe? How do you know?

3. Is Tom telling the story to Ellie? How do you know?

4. What changes would Tom make in his story if Joe or Ellie could hear him?

D. Sometimes we change what we say according to our audience. For example, we speak informally at home, but we speak formally to government officials. Informal letters are appropriate for our friends; on the other hand, letters to officials or for business purposes should be more formal in language. Even when we are speaking informally to our friends, we may not say exactly what we think. Sometimes in an attempt to influence the listener or reader, or to avoid being impolite, we don't communicate our point of view accurately and honestly.

Complete the following.

Example:

Situation	*Blunt Response*	*Tactful Response*
Tom is at Joe's house. Joe's dog bounces into the room, leaps up on Tom's lap, and licks his face.	Tom says, "Take that dog out of here. I hate dogs. They make me sneeze."	Tom says, "What a playful dog! He certainly is friendly. He must be a wonderful pet for your children. I'm sorry I'm too tired to play with him tonight." or "I am sorry I am allergic to dogs. I'd like to play with this one."

Situation	*Blunt Response*	*Tactful Response*
1. Joe has been out with Tom for two hours, leaving Ellie with the children on the night she usually goes to her League of Women Voters meeting. Ellie resents missing the meeting. Joe and Tom return to Joe's house.	Ellie says, "__________ __________ __________ __________ __________."	Ellie says, "__________ __________ __________ __________ __________."

2. Joe brings out several photograph albums to show Tom.	Tom says, "________ ________ ________ ________ ________."	Tom says, "________ ________ ________ ________ ________."
3. Joe asks Tom if he had any trouble recognizing him at the station.	Tom says, "________ ________ ________ ________."	Tom says, "________ ________ ________ ________."
4. Joe suggests that Tom stay overnight.	Tom replies, " ________ ________ ________ ________ ________ ________."	Tom replies, " ________ ________ ________ ________ ________ ________."

Look at each of your answers. Is Tom honest or dishonest in each? Is it possible to be honest and tactful at the same time? Are tactful answers always dishonest?

Exercise 4: Oral Practice

A. Use the correct word form.

Examples:

disappoint — The town was *disappointing,* according to Tom.
Tom was *disappointed.*

disgust — Dogs are *disgusting,* according to Tom.
Tom was *disgusted* by his trip.

Unit 7
Reading

bore disappoint	1. Tom thought the trip was ______________ and ______________.
surprise disgust	2. He was ______________ at the ______________ changes he found in his hometown.
interest	3. He is ______________ in architecture, but the most ______________ example in the town had been destroyed.
amaze confuse puzzle	4. The ______________ parking lot attendant was ______________ by Tom's ______________ behavior.
frighten entertain	5. Tom doesn't think dogs are ______________, but he isn't ______________ by their playful antics.

B. 1. Complete the following sentences.

The city used to have ______________, but it doesn't anymore.

______________,

______________,

The city used to have ______________ in the past, and it still does.

____

____

Joe used to like ______________, and he still does.

______________,

______________,

Tom used to dislike ______________, and he still does.

______________,

2. Practice using the following expressions.

used to

still

anymore

in the past

Example:

Tom used to like chocolate cake, and he still does.

Tom didn't like dogs in the past, and he still doesn't.

Use the above expressions to make complete sentences for the following:

__________ send Tom a Christmas photograph __________

__________ live in Tom's hometown __________

__________ live on Church Street __________

__________ go to the Home Bakery Coffee Shop on Saturdays __________

__________ like photography __________

__________ be bald __________

__________ look like a warehouse __________

__________ be allergic to dogs __________

__________ be friends with Tom __________

__________ dance at the Railway Hotel __________

__________ compete with the other stores __________

__________ be near the station __________

__________ like children __________

__________ be a four-lane highway __________

__________ have happy memories of his old town __________

__________ drink coffee __________

__________ be interested in architecture __________

C. Practice sentences using the present perfect with *since* and *for* ____.

Examples:

Joe liked Tom when they were boys.

Joe still likes Tom now.

Joe has liked Tom since they were boys.

Joe has liked Tom since boyhood.

Joe has liked Tom for many years.

---

1. Joe owned a camera in 1960.

   Joe still owns the same camera.

   ______________________________.

2. Tom was allergic to dog hair in his childhood.

   Tom is still allergic to dog hair.

   ______________________________.

3. Tom was interested in architecture in high school.

   Tom is an architect today.

   __________ has been __________ since __________.

4. Joe took his first family photograph thirty years ago.

   Joe still takes family photographs.

   ______________________________ for __________.

5. The coffee shop was sold five years ago.

   The coffee shop was boarded up five years ago.

   The coffee shop is still boarded up.

   ______________________________.

D. Change the following active sentences to passive.

Examples:

Joe takes a lot of photographs every year.

A lot of photographs are taken every year.

Joe sent Christmas cards to his friends last year.

Christmas cards were sent to Joe's friends last year.

Christmas cards were sent by Joe last year.

---

1. Joe entertained Tom.

   Tom ______________________________ by Joe.

2. Joe persuaded Tom to look at his photographs.

   Tom ______________________________ .

3. Joe met Tom at the station.

   Tom ______________ at the station by ______________ .

4. Tom interrupted Joe.

   ______________________________ .

5. Tom puzzled the parking lot attendant.

   ______________________________ .

E. Examine the following sentences. Indicate whether the sentence is active or passive.

Write the *other* form of the sentence.

Example:

Tom was invited to Joe's house. ______ *passive* ______

Joe invited Tom to his house.

---

1. The windows of the old store were boarded up by the new owner. ______________

   ______________________________ .

2. The old hotel with its old-fashioned architecture was torn down. ______________

   ______________________________ .

3. Tom forgot the name of his first date. ____________

____ .

4. The dog with the long hair annoyed Tom. ____________

____ .

5. A modern building had replaced the old school. ____________

____ .

6. The old church was destroyed by fire. ____________

____ .

7. Tom's suit was covered with dog hair. ____________

____ .

8. The city had built a new highway. ____________

____ .

9. Time had altered the old town. ____________

____ .

10. The hotel and coffee shop aren't visited by students anymore. ____________

____ .

Exercise 5: Logical Questions

A. Write appropriate questions for the following answers which are based on the story. All of the questions and answers are concerned with chronological order.

Example:

Has Tom recovered from his disappointment? Not yet.

	Question	*Answer*
1.	____?	Not anymore.
2.	____?	Yes, he used to.
3.	____?	No, he still doesn't.
4.	____?	Not yet.
5.	____?	Since childhood.
6.	____?	Until five years ago.

B. Write three questions of comparison based on the reading selection.

1. ____?

2. ____?

3. ____?

C. Write three questions of contrast about the reading selection.

1. ____?

2. ____?

3. ____?

D. Write appropriate questions for the following kinds of answers.

Example:

Question	Kind of Answer
How many kinds of changes did Tom find in his hometown?	Classification

	Question	*Kind of Answer*
1.	______________________________?	Reason
2.	______________________________?	Person
3.	______________________________?	Classification
4.	______________________________?	Number
5.	______________________________?	Spatial relationship

E. Write 4 questions of comparison and contrast which involve chronological order.

Use these patterns.

Contrast/Chronological Order

How was X different in the past from what *he, it, she, etc.* is like today?

How is X today different from what it used to be like?

In what ways was X's _______ in the past different from *its, her, his, etc.* _______ now?

In what ways is X's _______ today different from what it used to be like?

How did X differ in the past from what (*pronoun*) is like today?

How does X differ today from what it used to be like?

Comparison/Chronological Order

How was X in the past like X is today?

How was X in the past the same as X is today?

In what ways was X's _______ in the past {similar to / like / the same as} *its, her, his, etc.* _____ now?

How is X now like X used to be?

How is X now the same as X used to be?

1. ____?

2. ____?

3. ____?

4. ____?

Exercise 6: Descriptive Words

English has many descriptive words to express actions and appearances. For example, Tom *glowered* at the parking lot attendant. He *hurried on.* He *strode off,* but Joe *puffed along.*

1. What is the difference in meaning between these two sentences?

   Tom strode off.

   Tom walked away.

2. What is the difference in meaning between these two sentences?

   Joe puffed along.

   Joe walked along.

3. What is the difference in meaning among these three sentences?

   Tom glowered at him.

   Tom stared at him.

   Tom looked at him.

4. What does Tom mean by *the bosom of Joe's family?* Why did he choose this expression?

   ____

5. Why does Tom say Joe's pictures usually show a *droopy* Christmas tree?

   ____

6. Why does Tom call Joe a *boyhood pal* instead of *a friend?* Is this formal or informal language?

   ____

7. Why does Tom say Joe has *a crowd of children?*

   ____

8. Tom *interrupted* Joe. Tom *insisted* that they see the city. Why does he use these words instead of *said?* What do they tell us about Tom's character?

   ____

9. Why does the story say that the parking lot *stretched* where the old hotel used to be?

   ____

10. Explain what *merely shrugged his shoulders* means.

    ____

Conversation Practice

Several weeks after Tom's visit to his old hometown, he received a phone call from Joe.

1. Complete the following dialog.
2. After your teacher has checked it, practice your dialog with a partner. Later, you may want to "perform" it for your classmates.
3. Ask your classmates to decide whether Tom is rude or tactful, honest or dishonest in your dialog.

Tom: Hello.

Joe: Hi there, Tom. Guess what? I'm driving over to see you tomorrow. Be prepared for a big surprise.

Tom (politely): ______________________________

____

Joe: You certainly will be glad to see me especially when you see the surprise I'm bringing you.

Tom (tactfully): I just love surprises, but maybe you could give me a tiny clue about this one.

Joe: I think I should. Ellie said not to tell you ahead of time, but you may want to go out and get a dish and some puppy food, or . . . .

Tom (interrupts Joe): ______________________________

____

Joe: ______________________________

____

Tom: ______________________________

____

Joe: ______________________________

____

Writing

Exercise 1: Writing Sentences

A. Write 3 sentences which are true using *since.*

1. ______________________________ since he was a boy.

2. ______________________________ since high school.

3. ____________________ since the construction company destroyed the old hotel.

B. Write three sentences which are false using *used to.*

1. __________ used to __________, but __________ .

2. __________ used to __________, and __________ .

3. __________ used to __________, but nowadays __________

______________________________ .

C. Combine each of the following pairs of sentences to make one sentence. You may change the form of the original sentences.

Your sentences should be: chronological order
cause and result
comparison
contrast

Indicate what kind of sentence you have written. Circle the vocabulary which shows what kind of sentence you have written.

Example:

Tom began to feel disappointed.

Tom visited the familiar places of his youth.

Tom began to feel disappointed (while) he was visiting the familiar places of his youth.   *Chronological Order*

1. Tom glared angrily at the attendant in the parking lot.

   The destruction of the old hotel made Tom angry.

____

______________________________ __________

2. The distinguished visitor was very insistent.

   The hostess hesitated to refuse the request of the distinguished visitor.

   ____

   ______________________________ ______________

3. The construction company owner was tactless in his youth.

   The owner of the construction company always speaks bluntly and rudely to his employees.

   ____

   ______________________________ ______________

4. The church burned down.

   The church was well attended when it was first built.

   ____

   ______________________________ ______________

5. The small firm was profitable for several years in the 1950s.

   The small independent firm can't compete with large corporations today.

   ____

   ______________________________ ______________

Compare your answers with those of the other students. Is there more than one correct answer for some of the combined sentences?

Exercise 2: Writing about Information—Chronological Order, Comparison and Contrast

A. 1. Examine the following application form which was filled in by Joe.

CENTRAL STATE COLLEGE
Application Form

Personal Information

Name (in full)
Miss ______ Date January 4, 1975
Mrs. ______ Social Security No. 072-38-5493
Mr. Joseph P. Shields

Local address 316 (No.) North Elm (Street) Riverdale (City) Phone No. (310) 922-6178

Permanent address same (No. Street City) Phone No. same

Place of birth Riverdale (optional) Date of birth 3/14/30 Married or single? married

Widow or widower? no Separated or divorced? no Children (No.) 5

Ages? 2, 3, 5, 9, 12 American citizen? yes

Physical handicaps or disability none

Height 5′ 9″ Weight 205 lbs.

Position for which I am applying assistant professor of mechanical engineering

My major interest is in the teaching of mechanical engineering and anti-pollution control

I would accept a position teaching mechanical engineering, photography

Minimum salary I would accept $18,000

Earliest date available February 1, 1975

EDUCATION

	School	From	To	Certificate Diploma, Degree	Date
Secondary	Riverdale High School	1944	1947	diploma	1947
College, Univ. or specialized school	City Technological Institute, Riverdale	1950	1956	B.S.	1956
Graduate Work	Central State College	1958	1960	M.S.	1960
Honorary Degrees					

Academic Specialization

1. Undergraduate: Major fields of study: mathematics and engineering

   Minor fields of study: photography

2. Graduate: Major fields of special study: mechanical engineering

   Other fields of advanced study

3. Thesis subject: M.S. Pollution Control in Experimental Cars

   Ph.D.

Scholastic honors (prizes, honorary societies, etc.) photography prize from Riverdale High School, 1947

EXPERIENCE, beginning with most recent:

Dates	Firm or Institution	Salary	Position
1970 to present	City Technological Institute	$13,700	teacher of mechanical engineering
1968–1970	Riverdale Computer Co.	$12,000–12,400	engineer
1960–68	Shields Experimental Car Co.	$10,000 per year average	self-employed engineer in my own company. Company failed in 1968 due to competition from large corporations.

Hobbies: photography, dogs, local history

Travel: France, Germany, Switzerland in 1957

Record in Armed Services: in army from 1948 to 1950

Reason for leaving present position: higher salary

2. Make inferences about Joe on the basis of this information.

   a. In my opinion, Joe ______________________________.

   b. Joe's company must have been ______________________________.

   c. On the basis of his ____________________, I ____________________

   hire Joe because ______________________________.

3. The data implies some comparisons and contrasts about Joe's life.

   a. How is Joe's life as an adult similar to his life as a boy?

   ____________________ used to ____________________, and

   ____________________ still ____________________.

   b. In what ways has Joe's life changed? How is it different now from his life in the past?

   ____________________ used to ____________________;

   however, ______________________________.

4. Do you think employers should be allowed to ask personal questions concerning race, sex, marital status, age, or physical disabilities? Discuss with your classmates.

5. Use the information on the application form, your inferences, and what you know about Joe from the reading selection to write a composition about Joe's life. Compare and contrast Joe's life now with his life in the past.

   a. Make a list of ideas first.

Similarities	*Differences*
__________	__________
__________	__________
__________	__________
__________	__________
__________	__________
__________	__________

   b. Use vocabulary of chronological order, comparison and contrast.
   In many respects, my friend Joe's life has remained unchanged from the past; on the other hand, it

B. It is 1990; you have just returned to your old high school. Write a short composition in which you compare and contrast education in your youth with education "today." (Note: now = 1990.)

1. Make two lists of ideas first: one list for 1990 and the other for your own high school.

2. Divide your ideas into similarities and differences.

3. Use vocabulary of chronological order, comparison, and contrast.

I recently returned to my old high school which I haven't visited for more than ____________ years. In some respects, education today in 1990 is similar to mine; but in many areas the most amazing changes have taken place.

Exercise 3: Writing from Different Points of View

Several years ago the Home Bakery Coffee Shop had difficulty competing with the chain stores. It was still open, but business was bad.

A. You are the owner of the coffee shop. You are depressed about the failure of your business and worried about the future. Write a paragraph in which you contrast what your shop used to be like and what it is like now. (Now = several years ago before the business failed.)

I used to be one of the happiest men in town, but nowadays I ____________________. I can't compete with ____________________ anymore, and my profits ____________________ since five years ago. Then, ____.

On the other hand, ____.

I think ____.

In other words, ____.

B. Write another paragraph from the point of view of the wealthy businesswoman who wants to buy the property cheaply. She intends to buy several failing businesses in the area in order to make a profit.

Exercise 4: Capitalization

A. Examine the following sentences.

1. Mayor John F. Christianson, Jr., mayor of a large midwestern city and former head of Christianson Architectural Designs, Inc., is a distinguished Canadian alumnus of Central State College, which is near the Crystal River.

2. My friend, a vice-president of an architectural business, is a distinguished Canadian alumnus of a small college near a well-known river.

What is the rule for capitalizing titles of persons?

____

What is the rule for the capitalization of names of businesses?

____

What is the rule for capitalizing the names of rivers, lakes, mountains, etc.?

____

What is the rule for capitalizing the names of schools, hospitals, colleges, libraries, buildings, etc.?

____

What is the rule for names of countries and nationalities?

____

B. Look at earlier units.

1. What is the rule for capitalizing titles of books? Which words are usually not capitalized in titles of books and periodicals?

   ____

2. What is the rule for capitalizing the names of months, and the days of the week?

   ____

3. What is the rule for the names of languages?

   ____

4. What is the rule for the names of streets?

   ____

C. Punctuate the following sentences. Try to remember the rules from previous lessons.

1. after professor cameron graduated from college he taught french spanish and economics however nowadays he specializes in american economics and no longer teaches languages

2. john jay high school on south kennedy avenue is the oldest high school in the city however it is still the best

3. crystal river used to be crystal clear in former days but since 1970 it has been so polluted by the neighboring chemical factories that its name is no longer appropriate

4. because i love italian food i frequently eat at a small restaurant called marios on the main street of my hometown

5. mr mcwilliams the secretary announced politely president watson will interview you now in the treasurers office

Exercise 5: Point of View

Several months after his disappointing visit to his hometown, Thomas F. O'Brien received in the mail an invitation to be the vice-chairman of the alumni committee of his high school, which was planning a reunion to honor distinguished alumni of the school. The invitation was written by the chairman, Mr. John A. Hoover, Jr., a former classmate of Tom's, who had acquired a fortune in construction.

It was obvious from the tone of the letter that Mr. Hoover considered himself one of the school's distinguished alumni whom the reunion would honor, and that he was looking forward to the publicity the event would generate. John A. Hoover Enterprises was a building company with which Tom had tried unsuccessfully to get an architectural contract for years. He reasoned that work on the reunion committee might lead to future contracts, particularly if he was an efficient and innovative planner.

Write Tom's letter of acceptance to Mr. Hoover, including in the letter some suggestions for the reunion calculated to impress the committee chairman.

Tom's address ↗ ________________
↘ ________________

Date → ________________

________________ ← Mr. Hoover's full name

________________ ← Name of Hoover's firm

Dear Sir:

Sincerely yours,

Tom's full name → ________________

Exercise 6: Point of View and Paraphrase

A. As vice-chairman of the reunion planning committee, Tom had to revisit his hometown to make arrangements. While there, he was interviewed by the press. Complete the interview. Before you write the interview, consider the attitude Tom might have, and whether he should give his sincere opinions or not. Will he be honest, blunt, tactful, dishonest? Decide before you write.

Reporter: Mr. O'Brien, tell us something about yourself–background information, you know.

Answer (modestly): ____________________

____

Reporter: Where were you born?

Answer: ____________________

____

Reporter: What happy memories do you have of your school days here, Mr. O'Brien?

Answer: ____________________

____

Reporter: Which distinguished alumni do you plan to honor? Or is that a secret?

Answer: ____________________

____

Reporter: I'm from the local weekly newspaper. I'd like your impressions of our town now that you've returned after twenty years or so: what has been improved, what you miss, and so on.

Answer: ____________________

____

B. The local weekly newspaper reported this interview. Complete the newspaper article. Base "your" article on Tom's responses. Do not quote *verbatim* from the interview; paraphrase Tom's comments and use reported speech.

FORMER STUDENT ANNOUNCES REUNION PLANS

Plans were announced today for a gala reunion of distinguished alumni of our fine city high school. On hand to answer reporters' questions was Mr. Thomas O'Brien, vice-chairman of the high school alumni planning committee. Mr. O'Brien responded to questions about the reunion plans, and about his own reactions to the dramatic changes that have taken place here since his graduation. ____________________

____

____

____

____

Exercise 7: Personal Opinion—Anecdotes

A. Complete the following paragraph which starts with a generalization. Explain why you agree or disagree with the generalization. You may want to use an anecdote as an example. An anecdote is a brief story which is interesting. Anecdotes are often humorous. Use vocabulary of cause and result, comparison, contrast.

Many people think that being tactful is more important than being honest. I ______________ (agree/disagree/agree in part) with this opinion. ______________

In summary, it is my opinion that ______________.

B. Write a short composition about friendship.

1. Start with a generalization.

When we are young, we think that our friendships will last forever, but we are frequently mistaken.

or

Friendships seldom last.

or

It is difficult/impossible/possible to remain good friends with a person we rarely see.

2. Explain your opinion of the generalization. Give examples from your own experience.

3. Use the following vocabulary.

since	anymore
used to	no longer
still	

___

___

___

___

___

___

___

___

___

___

___

___

___

___

___

___

___

___

___

C. In Tom's adolescence going to the coffee shop was like a community ritual. Many communities and families engage in activities which are like rituals. The activity is repeated at regular intervals and is similar each time. Family celebrations which take place on birthdays or on holidays are often like rituals.

Complete the following paragraph which starts with a generalization.

Explain your opinion. You may want to give examples from your own experience.

Use vocabulary of cause and result and chronological order.

Use words like:	since	anymore
	used to	no longer
	still	etc.

It is important for children to participate in family and community celebrations because it is through these rituals that they become part of society. I ______________________________
agree/disagree/agree in part

____

____

____

____

____

____

____

____

____

____

____

____

____

____

____

____

____

Extra Vocabulary and Writing Practice

Exercise 1: Vocabulary Review

A. Indicate which of the following terms are derogatory and which are favorable.

ugly	________________
polite	________________
tactful	________________
obliging	________________
boring	________________
hospitable	________________
sentimental	________________
fat	________________
handsome	________________
innovative	________________
distinguished	________________

B. Complete the following chart with the appropriate forms.

Noun	*Verb*
growth	________________
________________	interrupt
alteration	________________
________________	compete
replacement	________________
________________	improve
________________	build
disappearance	________________
________________	intend
disappointment	________________
________________	respond

invitation	____________
construction	____________
calculation	____________
reaction	____________
____________	honor
suggestions	____________
____________	accept

C. Complete the following with the appropriate forms.

Verb	*Adjective*
hesitate	____________
____________	insistent
____________	competitive
____________	confidential
differ	____________
____________	profitable

Exercise 2: Vocabulary and Spelling Review

1. As an arch_ _ _ _ _, Tom thought it was advisable for him to impr_ss the w_ _ _thy ch_ _ _man of the c_mm_ _ _ee.

2. Tom wr_ _ _ his letter of _ _ _ _ _tance in for_ _ _ l_ _ _ _ _ge.

3. Tom expl_ _ _ _ _ to the newspaper re_ _ _ _er the reasons for the reunion and tact_ _ _ _ _ summarized his im_ _ _ _ _ions of his _ _ _ _town.

4. Because Joe's hobby is ph_ _ _ _ _ _phy, Tom ex_ _ _ _ _ him to take a lot of p_ _ _ _ _ _ _ of his former cl_ _ _ _ _ _ _ _ at the re_ _ _ _ _.

5. Re_ _ _ _ing to a place of which we have happy m_ _ _ _ies is often very dis_ _ _ _ _ _ _ _ _ _.

Exercise 3: Compositions

A. Most people change as they grow older. They change in their appearance and in their likes and dislikes. Describe a person you have known for a number of years. Tell how he has changed and how he has remained the same.

1. Make a list of ideas first. Organize your list into similarities and differences.

2. Start your composition with a chronological statement and a generalization of comparison and contrast. (Note that this generalization is also classification.)

   I have known ______________________ since ______________________________ . In several

   ______________________ ways he has changed, but in several ______________________ ways he is
   significant/insignificant significant/insignificant
   still the same.

3. Give examples. Tell anecdotes (personal stories).

4. After your story is finished, check your verb tenses.

B. Tom was disappointed because his expectations were not fulfilled. Describe an experience in which you were disappointed.

1. Start with the following generalization.

   Expectation is often better than realization.

2. Next give example(s) from your own life.

   A disappointing experience from my life proves this.

   or

   Let me cite a personal experience as proof.

3. Tell your story in chronological order.

4. Contrast what you expected and what happened. Use appropriate vocabulary.

C. Describe a place where you used to live of which you have happy memories.

or

Describe an activity or hobby you used to like, but that you don't have time for any more.

or

Describe the town in which you grew up.

D. Describe the most boring evening you have spent.

or

Describe a family you never want to meet/visit again.

E. Describe the most important changes that have taken place in your country in the last ten years.

1. Make a list first.
2. Organize your list into different kinds of changes.
3. Start with a generalization of classification.
4. Give examples. Contrast the past and the present.
5. When your composition is finished, check your tenses.

F. Many people believe that it is better not to return to the place of one's childhood because going back is always a disappointment. Do you agree?

Write a composition to explain your point of view.

1. Start with a generalization. You may want to use the generalization given at the beginning of this exercise (F).

   Many people believe that returning to one's hometown (birthplace, old school, etc.) is bound to be a disappointment. I agree/disagree/agree in part for ______________________ reasons.

2. Give your reasons. Use examples, and/or anecdotes.
3. Your composition will combine: generalization and examples
   cause and result
   classification

   It will probably also include some: comparison
   contrast
   chronological order

   Use appropriate vocabulary.

Unit 8: Reading

Appearances Count

It was raining hard, and Joe's long black hair was thoroughly soaked by the time he arrived home. He threw his school books on the hall table, draped his wet jacket over a chair, and stamped into the kitchen.

"Wipe your feet." His mother's greeting was automatic as she stooped to remove a roast from the oven. Glasses blotted with steam, she wiped her face with her checked apron. "You'd better dry your hair. Not here, though. No long hairs in the mashed potatoes in my house."

"Right enough. That's the trouble with the young people nowadays. Too much hair, too little hard work." Joe's grandfather chuckled. "Why don't you carry an umbrella? When I was your age, we. . . ."

Joe left the kitchen before the old man could finish. "Stupid old bore," he muttered.

That night at dinner as the rain ran down the windows in silver-gray streams, obscuring the leafless trees and the emptied swimming pool, the family discussed in a desultory way what they might do the following summer. Joe's father, who was a firm believer in planning ahead, had already been to three travel agents for brochures. Joe's mother was always content to allow her husband to make the final decisions, but the children were not usually so agreeable. Joe's younger sister, Beth, cared only about one thing this year: horses. She refused to go anywhere if she couldn't ride. She'd rather die, she announced dramatically. Joe's other sister, Cathy, had no intention of going anywhere. She was going to get a job to earn money for medical school.

"Good idea," Joe's father said. "Why don't you get a job too, son? It would teach you to be independent. Maybe Pa could fix you up with a job at the bank. What do you think, Pa?"

The old man chuckled, "Fix him up all right; yes, I'll fix him up. First, he'll get a haircut. Next, he'll polish his shoes, put on a suit, a white shirt, and a tie. Then, we'll consider an interview. Appearances count in the business world, young man. Appearances count."

"Stupid old bore," Joe said aside to Cathy as he pushed his chair back abruptly and stamped out of the dining room.

The rainy night was followed by a foggy half-lit morning. Joe's gloomy mood matched the atmosphere outside the classroom windows. The teacher, young, enthusiastic, was trying without much success to interest the students in folk tales. The story under discussion concerned a young man who, having acquired much wealth, returned to his native land only to find it under the control of an extremely greedy tyrant.

"How can he fulfill his wish to be an important man in his own country? Any ideas? What would you do if you were the young man?" The teacher's questions seemed to Joe as unreal as the foggy world outside. "What a bore!" he whispered to himself.

The teacher read aloud.

> Two days later he stood before the greedy king. "Your Majesty, I have but one request to make of you. I wish to present to you all my vast wealth. To you I will give all my gold, my silver, my diamonds, my many fine horses, and one thousand precious rings." The king's eyes

glittered with greed. "In return for the honor of presenting you my unworthy wealth, I beg but one small favor. On the day of your birthday celebration, allow me to approach your most noble person and whisper in your ear."

On the day of the king's birthday, the noble guests were astonished to see a stranger approach the king and whisper in his ear. From that day forth, although his wealth was now the king's, the young man was so well regarded by all the citizens that he became famous and influential throughout the land.

"What relevance does this story have for us today?" Joe jumped; the question was for him. The teacher smiled expectantly as Joe scraped his feet, and twisted a strand of long black hair. To his utter amazement, he heard his voice. "Appearances count?" The teacher nodded enthusiastically. Joe stared at his feet, frowning. "What a bore!" he thought.

Exercise 1: Reading for Information

A. Indicate whether the following sentences are true or false according to the story, or whether you have insufficient information to reach a decision. Be prepared to explain your answer.

Example:

Whenever it rains, Joe carries an umbrella. ______ *false* ______

1. Joe's mother knows how Joe behaves whenever it rains. ____________
2. In spite of his attitude, Joe is influenced by his grandfather's ideas. ____________
3. Joe's parents are not very strict with their children. ____________
4. Joe's grandfather is critical of Joe but in a friendly way. ____________
5. The story takes place during the summer. ____________
6. Although Joe's family isn't poor, they aren't extremely wealthy either. ____________
7. Joe's grandfather used to work in a bank. ____________
8. Joe's older sister wishes she were a horse. ____________
9. Joe is the oldest child in the family, and he's the rudest too. ____________
10. Joe's younger sister isn't as interested in clothes as her mother wants her to be. ____________
11. Cathy's likes and dislikes change from year to year. ____________
12. Joe's behavior is consistent. ____________

B. On the basis of the *implicit* and *explicit* information in the reading selection do you agree or disagree with the following statements? Explain your answer.

1. Joe's grandfather wishes his grandson were more like the boys of his own youth.

   ____

2. Cathy wishes her family would take their vacation on a ranch.

   ____

3. Cathy's sister wishes she had richer parents.

   ____

4. Joe's mother wishes Joe were less careless and more polite to his elders.

   ____

5. The English teacher wishes the students were as enthusiastic as she is about literature.

   ____

6. If the weather improves, the students will be more attentive.

   ____

7. If the family goes to the ocean for their vacation, the younger daughter won't die.

   ____

8. If the parents were stricter with their children, Joe wouldn't be so bored.

   ____

9. If Joe worked in the bank, he would be happy.

   ____

10. If Joe had worked in the bank last year, he would have been a good worker because his behavior is consistent.

    ____

Exercise 2: Descriptive Language

Descriptive words are sometimes used by writers to give explicit information about people, places, or actions. Descriptive language is also sometimes used to imply additional information. The reading selection in this unit uses descriptive language to convey both explicit and implicit information.

A. 1. What descriptive words in the first paragraph of the reading selection tell you about Joe's behavior?

______________ ______________ ______________

2. What inference do you make about Joe's attitude based on these words?

____

3. What is the difference in meaning between:

stamped and *walked?*

draped and *hung?*

4. Find other descriptive words which imply information about Joe's attitude.

______________ ______________ ______________

5. Joe's mother's greeting was *automatic.* What does that imply about her? about Joe?

____

6. What kind of a person is Joe's grandfather? The story doesn't tell us explicitly. Find a descriptive word or phrase which implies what kind of person he is.

____

7. What is the difference in meaning between:

mutter and *say?*

whisper to himself and *say* something *aside* to somebody?

8. The discussion was *desultory?* What does this imply?

____

B. 1. The author of this reading selection uses words and phrases to describe the weather. Find the descriptive phrases which describe the evening and the next morning.

________________ ________________ ________________

2. Explain what is meant by:

half-lit morning ________________

gloomy atmosphere ________________

unreal as the foggy world outside ________________

leafless trees ________________

silver-grey streams ________________

3. What is the difference in meaning between:

wet and *soaked?*

covered and *blotted?*

large and *vast?*

4. The author compares Joe's mood to the weather outside. What phrases does she use?

____

____

Is this effective? Why?

____

C. Which person in the story would you use each of the following words to describe?

Example:

greedy ___*the king*___

---

insistent ________________

enthusiastic ________________

tactful ________________

rude ________________

careless ________________

agreeable ________________

athletic ____________________

ambitious ____________________

hesitant ____________________

ingenious ____________________

bored ____________________

cheerful ____________________

boring ____________________

inconsiderate ____________________

efficient ____________________

old-fashioned ____________________

critical ____________________

impatient ____________________

Exercise 3: Reading for Inferences about Logical Relationships

A. The reading selection is a narrative told in chronological sequence. Within the larger narrative there is a short narrative (the folk tale) which is also told in chronological order. Although the overall organization of the story is chronological order, the story includes comparison and contrast explicitly and implicitly.

1. Find two explicit examples of comparison or contrast in the story.

   a. ____________________

   b. ____________________

2. The story implies comparison and contrast about the members of the family.

   a. What contrast can you make between the mother and father?

   ____________________; however ____________________.

   b. Make an inference of contrast about the two sisters and their brother.

   ____________________; on the other hand, ____________________.

c. Make an inference of comparison between one sister and the brother.

____ ;

similarly, ____________________________________ .

d. Make an inference of contrast about the mother and her two daughters.

Although ____________________________________ ,

____ .

B. Examine the following sentences.

Despite the teacher's enthusiasm, the students were bored.

In spite of the teacher's enthusiasm, the students were bored.

Although his grandfather was an experienced businessman, Joe did not treat him with respect.

Despite his grandfather's experience in business, Joe did not treat him respectfully.

In spite of his grandfather's business experience, Joe did not behave respectfully toward him.

1. Give the rules for sentence patterns with:

although

despite

in spite of

2. Are the above sentences comparison or contrast?

3. Complete the following.

The teacher was ______________________________ ; on the other hand,

____________________ the students ____________________ .

Although the students ____________________ , ____________________

____ .

Joe's grandfather had a lot of ______________________________ , but

____________________________________ respect him.

Although Joe ____________________ , ____________________ .

4. Contrast this pair of sentences.

   The teacher was enthusiastic, but the students were bored.

   Although the teacher was enthusiastic, the students were bored.

   Both the sentences make a contrast. However, in the sentence with *although,* the writer is giving us some additional information. The use of *although* indicates to us that we would normally expect a different cause and result relationship. Normally, we would expect the students to be enthusiastic too *because* the teacher is enthusiastic.

Additional Vocabulary of Contrast
Although Despite —— In spite of ——

Use this contrast vocabulary for contrast which also indicates an unexpected cause and result.

C. Read the following sentences. Indicate for each whether the sentence is:

   contrast

   cause and result

   contrast and chronological order

   contrast which indicates unexpected cause and result.

Example:

He used to be polite, but he isn't anymore. *contrast and chronological order*

---

1. Some parents are too permissive; on the other hand, others are overly strict with their children. ____________

2. The mother anticipated the child's behavior, so her response was automatic. ____________

3. Although Joe was irritated by his grandfather's comments, he was influenced by them. ____________

4. According to the old man, boys behaved more responsibly in the past than they do today. ____________

5. In spite of his critical attitude, Joe's grandfather is really very fond of him. ____________

6. The English class was so dull that the students thought literature was irrelevant to their lives. ____________

Exercise 4: Hypothesis

One major kind of inference which English speakers frequently use is hypothesis, in other words, inferences using *if.* Hypotheses indicate a special kind of cause and result relationship.

Possibility:

If she earns a lot of money, = She might . . . .

Contrary to fact:

If he studied, = He doesn't study.

If he had studied, = He didn't study.

A. Examine the following inferences which use *if.* Indicate if the sentence is *a real possibility* or *contrary to fact.*

Example:

If Cathy earns a lot of money, she will go to medical school. *real possibility*

---

1. If Joe studied harder, he would get better grades. ____________
2. If Joe had taken an umbrella to school, he wouldn't have been so wet. ____________
3. If the younger sister gets a horse, she will be happy. ____________
4. If Joe follows his father's advice, he will get a job at the bank. ____________
5. If Joe had followed his grandfather's advice, he would have changed his appearance. ____________

In English sentences, *if* implies real possibility or an idea which is contrary to fact.

B. 1. What are the grammar rules for hypotheses which are true now and in the future? What verb forms are correct?

If clause ____________________

Main clause ____________________

2. What are the grammar rules for hypotheses which are contrary to fact now, or likely to be contrary to fact in the future?

If clause ____________________

Main clause ____________________

3. What are the grammar rules for hypotheses which are contrary to fact in the past?

If clause ____________________

Main clause ____________________

C. It is often useful to make inferences of cause and result which involve hypothetical situations. For example, scientists frequently use hypotheses in planning experiments; city managers, businessmen, economists, and politicians must use hypotheses in planning for the future; people use hypotheses in everyday life to plan their budgets and their time. Based on the reading selection, make three inferences of hypothesis of the following kind.

1. topic: the family vacation

   kind of inference: a real possibility now and in the future.

   If ______________________________, ______________________________________.

2. topic: the season

   kind of sentence: contrary to fact now

   If ______________________________, ______________________________________.

3. topic: the folk tale

   kind of inference: contrary to fact in the past

   If ______________________________, ______________________________________.

Hypothesis Additional Vocabulary of Cause and Result
if ______
unless ___ (= if & not)

Use *if* for real possibility or hypothesis which is contrary to fact.

Exercise 5: Oral Practice

A. 1. Complete the following using *in spite of.*

In spite of the rain, he didn't carry an umbrella.

the season, ______________________________ plan his vacation.

the criticism, Joe ______________________________ .

the students' boredom, the teacher ______________________________ .

the teacher's enthusiasm, ______________________________ were bored.

the greedy king, the young man ______________________________ .

2. Use the same ideas as in the oral practice above, but use *although.*

Example:

Although it was raining, he didn't carry an umbrella.

Although ____________________, ____________________ plan his vacation.

Although ____________________ was critical, Joe ____________________ .

Although the students were ____________________, the teacher ____________________

Although the teacher was ____________________, ____________________ .

Although the king ____________________, ____________________ .

B. Practice the following sentences with *wish.*

1. a. The younger daughter wants a horse.
   b. She wishes she had a horse.

2. a. The employer wants the boy to have short hair.
   b. He wishes the boy had short hair.

3. a. The student wants the lesson to end.
   b. ____________________ wishes ____________________ was/were over.

4. a. The teacher wants the class to be enthusiastic.
   b. ____________________ wishes ____________________ enthusiastic.

5. a. The girl wants enough money to become a doctor.
   b. ____________________ wishes ____________________

6. a. The ambitious young man wants to be famous.
   b. The ambitious young man wishes he ____________________ .

C. Complete the following sentences with *wish.*

1. Teenage boys are often impatient with their elders, but their parents ______________________.
2. The student doesn't know the answer, but he ______________________.
3. The teacher can't make the students enthusiastic about folk lore, but ______________________.
4. Foggy and rainy weather depresses Joe, so he wishes ______________________.
5. The king is a greedy tyrant; therefore, his subjects wish ______________________.

D. Practice the following patterns using *if.*

1. She will earn a lot of money if she gets a job.

She will earn	a lot of money if she	gets	a job.
would		got	
would have earned		had got (gotten)	

2. He will get a haircut if he works at the bank.

He will	get a haircut if he	works	at the bank.
would		________	
_____		had worked	

3. He will be happy if he follows his grandfather's advice.

He will be	happy if he	follows	his grandfather's advice.
__________		followed	
would have been		__________	

4. If the teacher is enthusiastic, the students will learn.

If the teacher	is	enthusiastic, the students	will learn.
	_____	,	would
	had been	,	__________

5. If the weather improves, the citizens will be happy.

If the weather	improves	, the citizens	will be happy.
	improved	,	__________
	had improved	,	__________

6. If the king dies, the citizens will be happy.

If the king	dies	, the citizens	will be happy.
	_____	,	would be
	had died	,	__________

E. Practice *unless* and *if* patterns.

1 a Unless he works, he won't earn any money.

b. If he doesn't work, he won't earn any money.

2. a. Unless the weather changes, the alumni will be disappointed in the reunion.

b. If ______________________, ______________________.

3. a. Unless it costs him too much interest, the father will take out a loan in order to buy a horse for his daughter.

b. If ______________________, ______________________.

4. a. Unless the job interview is successful, the student will continue to depend on his family for money.

b. If ______________________, ______________________.

5. a. Unless ambitious citizens are as ingenious as the young man in the folk story, they will have difficulty in fulfilling their ambitions.

b. ______________________ if ______________________.

Exercise 6: Logical Questions

A. 1. The reading selection includes a folk story. Part of the folk story is summarized. Write questions about the folk story which the summary does not answer. Think about other information you would like to have. Your questions must conform to the *type* of answer indicated.

a. ______________________________? Name of a place

b. ______________________________? Date

c. ______________________________? Comparison

d. ______________________________? Reason

e. ______________________________? Classification

2. Write questions about the folk story that the teacher might ask the students. The question must correspond to the *type* of answer indicated.

a. ______________________________? Inference

b. ______________________________? Explicit information from the folk tale

c. ______________________________? Inference which is a generalization

d. ______________________________? Inference which is a contrast

e. ______________________________? Personal opinion

B. One of Joe's sisters intends to get a job to earn money. She is going to be interviewed by the supervisor of a small veterinary clinic.

Write three questions the employer will probably ask her.

1. ______________________________?

2. ______________________________?

3. If ______________, ______________?

Write three questions she should ask the employer.

1. ______________________________?

2. ______________________________?

3. If ______________, ______________?

Conversation Practice

Point of View

At the end of each semester, the teachers at the high school which Joe attends send a report to each student's parents about their child's progress and attitude. Joe's father has just received Joe's report from his English teacher.

Name of student: Joseph Robert Stowe

Name of Teacher: Mrs. Yvonne Mitchell

Subject: English (Junior year–World Literature)

Semester: First Year: 1975

Grade: C–

Comments: Joe's work this semester has been very disappointing. Although he has ability, his written work is careless. He seldom participates in class discussions. He is uncooperative and, on occasion, defiant. Both his work habits and his attitude need to improve. Please make an appointment with the school counselor.

Parent's Signature ____________________ Date __________

A. Complete the following conversation between Joe and his father.

Mr. Stowe (angrily): Just look at this report. What did I ever do to deserve a son like you? Your mother and I have given you everything you want, and how do you behave? You're careless. You're uncooperative. You're . . . .

Joe (interrupts him): Calm down. It's only a stupid old English class. If you had to sit through all that foolishness about poetry, and synonyms, and crazy stories, you'd be bored too. Besides, I do well in chemistry.

Mr. Stowe: Don't change the subject. Nobody cares whether you're bored. Your sisters aren't bored.

Joe (angrily): ____

____

Mr. Stowe: ____

____

Joe (defiantly): ____

____

Mr. Stowe: ____

____

Joe: ____

____

B. The next week Joe's father had an interview with the school's counselor.

1. Complete the following conversation. (Before you write, decide whether Joe's father will talk to the counselor the way he talks to Joe. Will he be tactful, rude, honest, cooperative, etc.? Will he defend Joe? Will the counselor be tactful? Will he find fault with Joe's father's attitude? etc.)

2. Read your dialog aloud with a classmate.

Counselor: Good afternoon. I'm very glad you could take time to talk to me. You see, we are worried about your son. He isn't fulfilling our expectations. In other words, he isn't stupid, but he isn't using his abilities.

Mr. Stowe: I understand what you mean, but I don't know what I can do. I've talked to him about his report, of course.

Counselor (tactfully): ______________________________

____

Mr. Stowe: ______________________________

____

Counselor: ______________________________

____

Mr. Stowe (abruptly): He says he's bored.

Counselor: ______________________________

____

Mr. Stowe: ______________________________

____

C. The counselor must keep a record of all his interviews with parents. He summarizes the main points of each interview immediately afterward. Because he doesn't take notes during the interview, he must paraphrase what was said. He also writes comments about his own reactions.

1. Paraphrase one of the interviews "performed" in class. Remember that your report must be from the counselor's point of view.

2. Assume you are the counselor. Add your own evaluation of the interview.

Counselor's Name:

Date:

Time:

Name of Parent:

Name of Student:

Summary of Interview:

____

____

____

____

____

____

____

Counselor's Comments:

____

____

____

____

____

____

____

____

Writing

Exercise 1: Writing Sentences

Write sentences based on the reading selection and the conversation practice situation. Your sentences must conform to the *kind* of sentence indicated.

1. ______________________________	Contrast
2. ______________________________ For example, ______________________________	Generalization and example
3. ______________________________ .	Classification
4. ______________________________ .	Cause and Result
5. ______________________________ .	Comparison
6. ______________________________ .	Chronological Order
7. ______________________________ ______________________________ .	Contrast and Chronological Order
8. ______________________________ ______________________________ .	Contrast with unexpected cause and result
9. Unless ______________________________ , ______________________________	Cause and result which is a real possibility
10. ______________________________ ______________________________	Hypothesis which is contrary to fact
11. In my opinion, ______________________________ , ______________________________	Contrast which includes personal opinion
12. ______________________________ in spite of ______________________________ .	Contrast with unexpected cause and result.

Exercise 2: Interpreting Information

In addition to traditional stories, such as folk tales, most cultures have traditional sayings which summarize basic beliefs in a few words.

A. 1. Consider the following sayings. Explain in your own words what each means.

Beauty is only skin deep.

You can't judge a book by its cover.

Appearances are deceiving.

Appearances count.

All that glitters is not gold.

2. Do they all mean the same?

3. In your opinion, which of these sayings apply to the folk tale?

Which of these might Joe use to contradict his grandfather's argument?

B. Complete the following paragraphs.

One possible interpretation of the folk tale is that appearances are important. For example, the young man's ______________________ was due to appearances. When the citizens ______________________, they thought that ______________________. If he hadn't ______________________ ______________________, he wouldn't have ______________________.

On the other hand, a different interpretation is also possible. Although the story illustrates that appearances can influence people, it also shows that appearances are deceiving. If the citizens had known ______________________ ______________________, they ______________________.

The young man was successful because he realized that ______________________ ______________________.

These two interpretations clearly show the value of folk tales and proverbs. Although such stories and sayings appear deceptively simple, they can convey ______________________ to both children and ______________________

C. Read the following short story.

The New Baby

"What a sweet, sweet baby! Who does he look like? He has blue eyes like his mother and dark hair like his father. He looks so innocent sleeping there."

Maryanne heard the voices clearly from the bottom of the stairs. Aunt Ellen and her mother were looking at the baby. The new baby was all anybody cared about anymore. Maryanne felt a tear trickling down her cheek. Last year she was Aunt Ellen's favorite, but not anymore. Aunt Ellen didn't even bother to ask where she was. She hurried upstairs just like everybody else to praise the new boy, the first boy in the family.

Maryanne sat on the bottom step and put her fingers in her ears. The baby was ugly with a red wrinkled face. He didn't have any teeth. He couldn't do anything worthwhile. All he could do was cry and sleep. He couldn't read or play the piano. What was so special about black hair? Maybe if her hair was black, they'd pay attention to her again. Maryanne got up, ran quickly into the kitchen and started to rub black shoe polish into her long blonde hair.

Use the following two sayings to interpret the events in the story.

Appearances count.

Appearances are deceiving.

1. How does Maryanne's behavior prove her belief in the idea that appearances are important?
2. How will the adults interpret her behavior?
3. In what way does the story illustrate the idea that appearances are deceiving?
4. Is Maryanne's interpretation of the situation accurate/too simple/too complicated?

D. Complete the following. Use ideas from the two reading selections and from your own experience.

Although we constantly make inferences about people from their appearance and their actions, it is not easy to avoid misinterpretations. This does not imply that we should never make inferences. For example, ________

____.

This kind of inference can be very useful. However, we must be very careful when we interpret another person's behavior. For example, if ____,

____. Many parents ____.

This can lead to misunderstanding. Teachers also ________________________________.

If ________________________, ________________________________.

Therefore, ____.

Exercise 3: Paraphrase

The folk tale in the reading selection is in two parts. The first section is a summary which tells briefly what the students have already read. The second part gives the story itself *verbatim,* including details and direct speech. Complete the following summary of the entire story. Paraphrase; do not copy, but give the information in your own words. Use reported speech rather than direct speech.

Long ago, an ambitious young boy of an obscure family left his home in order to seek his fortune. Before his departure, he vowed to return a wealthy man and to take his place among the most influential citizens of the land.

____

____

____

____

____

____

Exercise 4: Punctuating Clauses and Phrases

A. Examine the punctuation of the following sentences.

Although babies are very demanding, parents should not neglect older children.
Parents should not neglect older children although babies are very demanding.

If parents have one favorite child, the other children will be jealous.
The other children will be jealous if parents have one favorite child.

In spite of their good intentions, parents often teach their children to be uncooperative and disobedient.
Parents often teach their children to be uncooperative and disobedient in spite of their good intentions.

The rules for punctuating the following clauses and phrases are the same. Explain.

when ---	because ---	subsequent to ____
after ---	because of ____	if ---
before ---	unless ----	due to ____
prior to ____	despite ____	although ---

B. Punctuate the following sentences.

1. although some parents are affectionate to their children when they are infants they grow more and more hostile to them when they behave independently in adolescence

2. if parents are permissive children will become rebellious

3. although we can find examples of men and women who rose from obscure backgrounds to fame we cannot assume that ambition is always rewarded on the contrary these persons are exceptions to the rule

4. too much criticism can damage a childs self-respect therefore teachers and parents should be considerate when they discuss problems with children

5. some psychologists believe that unless children learn to compete with each other in childhood they will be unable to cope with the competition of the adult world

Exercise 5: Compositions of Hypothesis

Write compositions of hypothesis on the following topics. For each topic:

1. Make a list of ideas first.
2. Organize your ideas.
3. Start with a general statement.
4. Give more than one hypothetical example. Unless ____, ______. On the other hand, if _____,

   _______.
5. Use: *if, unless;* vocabulary of contrast; vocabulary of chronological order; vocabulary of cause and result.
6. After you have finished, check your verbs, especially in the sentences using *if.*

A. Joe's English teacher wants to send a copy of Joe's semester report to the businessman who is going to interview Joe for a summer job. If you were Joe's father, would you object? Why or why not?

B. Maryanne's parents were disappointed when she was born because they wanted a boy to carry on the family name and to inherit the family business. If you could give them some advice, what would you tell them? Why?

C. Joe's father contrasted Joe unfavorably with his sisters when they were discussing Joe's report. If you were a school counselor, what suggestions would you give parents about comparing and contrasting their children? Explain.

Exercise 6: Contrast—Personal Opinion

Write brief compositions to explain your opinion of *two* of the following statements, all of which are contrasts. Explain whether you agree, disagree, or agree only in part with each point of view. Give your reasons. Give examples and hypothetical situations using *if* and *unless.*

A. Considerate people are less likely to be successful than competitive people who aren't influenced by the feelings of others.

B. Although adults expect children to respect them, not all grownups have earned the right to the admiration and respect of the young.

C. Young people are often more influenced by the actions of adults than by their advice and warnings.

D. Although parents claim to love all their children equally, they usually have one favorite child.

E. It is more important to teach children that appearances are deceiving than to teach them that appearances are important.

Extra Vocabulary and Writing Practice

Exercise 1: Vocabulary Review

A. Complete the following chart with the appropriate word forms.

Noun	*Verb*	*Adjective*
respect	______	______
______	______	cooperative
______	______	influential
competition	______	______
______	______	permissive
______	expect	______
consideration	______	______

B. Complete the following with the appropriate word forms.

Noun	*Adjective*
______	famous
ambition	______
greed	______
ability	______
______	gloomy
attention	______
______	automatic
______	hypothetical
drama	______

C. Match the antonyms in the following lists.

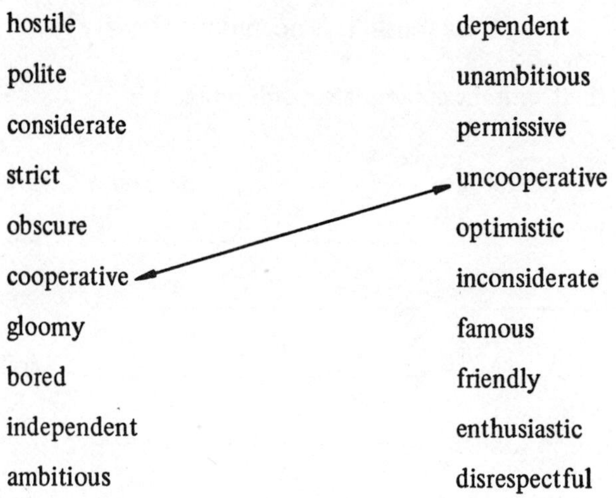

hostile	dependent
polite	unambitious
considerate	permissive
strict	uncooperative
obscure	optimistic
cooperative	inconsiderate
gloomy	famous
bored	friendly
independent	enthusiastic
ambitious	disrespectful

Exercise 2: Vocabulary and Spelling Review

1. Pa_____ sometimes exp___ their child___ to f__fill their own am___ions.

2. Al______ adol___ents often seem in___sid__ate and def____, they are us_al__ in___enced by the__ e__ers.

3. Am___ious people are fre_____ly com___itive and in__pend___; on the other h___, many un__bit____ people achieve suc____ through co__er_____.

4. Stu_____ who are b__ed are not nec___ar___ l_z_ and dis__spect___.

5. If we base our op_____s on ap______ces, we will be dec___ed, accor____ to many tr_d_tion__ s__ings.

Exercise 3: Compositions

A. The ambitious man in the folk tale wanted to be famous in his native land. If you could do anything you wished for one year in order to become famous in your native land, what would you do? Write a composition using chronological order and cause and result.

B. Describe a person who has had the greatest influence on your ideas or character. Start with a generalization. Give examples. Make inferences about your life if you had never met this person or if he/she had been different. Use chronological order, cause and result, contrast and comparison.

C. Do you think that parents should encourage their children to be competitive? Write a composition of personal opinion in which you compare and contrast the results of competition among children in the same family.

1. Make a list of advantages and disadvantages before you start. Organize your list into categories.

2. Start with a question.

   Should parents encourage their children to be competitive?

3. Follow the opening question with a generalization which is a statement of contrast.

   Although competition among children can be beneficial, it has many disadvantages.

   or

   In spite of a few disadvantages, competition among children is generally beneficial.

4. Explain your generalization using examples. Use vocabulary of comparison, contrast, cause and result. Use some sentences of hypothesis to explain your point of view.

D. In many countries elderly relatives live alone or in institutions rather than with their families. Do you approve or disapprove of this practice? What are the advantages and disadvantages of this practice?

Write a composition in which you explain your point of view.

1. Start with a question.

2. Follow your question with a generalization which is a statement of contrast.

3. Give examples and reasons. Use vocabulary of comparison, contrast, cause and result. Use some sentences with *if* and *unless*.

E. If you could tell only one story to your children in order to influence their characters, what story would you choose? Why?

1. Start with a generalization and a hypothesis.

Traditionally, children have been taught about ______________________________
good and evil/ambition/respect for their elders, etc.
through stories.

If I could tell only one story to my children, I would tell them _ _ _ _ _ _.

2. Summarize the story. Use chronological order. Use indirect speech.

3. Explain the reasons for your choice.